TO:

....

FROM:

....

100
devotions
for the
STAY-AT-HOME MOM

ZONDERVAN®

100 Devotions for the Stay-at-Home Mom

Copyright © 2023 Zondervan

Portions of this book were adapted from: *365 Devotions for Rest* and *365 Devotions for What Matters Most.*

Requests for information should be addressed to:

Zondervan, *3900 Sparks Dr. SE, Grand Rapids, Michigan 49546*

Zondervan titles may be purchased in bulk for educational, business, fundraising, or sales promotional use. For information, please email SpecialMarkets@Zondervan.com.

ISBN 978-0-7852-9335-4 (softcover)
ISBN 978-0-7852-9337-8 (audio)
ISBN 978-0-7852-9336-1 (ebook)

Cover design: Jamie DeBruyn

Interior design: Kristy Edwards

Printed in the United States of America
23 24 25 26 27 LBC 5 4 3 2 1

❦❦❦❦❦ Introduction ❦❦❦❦❦

other. Does any other word carry such weight and meaning behind it? Does any other word have the potential to absorb one's identity as much as this one? This can be especially true when your calling is to be a stay-at-home mom. Some think you relax all day (insert laughter here), but you know what is required of you. The physical and emotional labor you pour into your family every day sometimes goes unseen, unrecognized. But the Lord sees you. He sees you on days when all is going well: "She is clothed with strength and dignity; she can laugh at the days to come" (Proverbs 31:25). And He sees you on the days where you need as much comfort as your children: "As a mother comforts her child, so will I comfort you" (Isaiah 66:13).

In the midst of being a stay-at-home mom, and all that that encompasses, are you making time for self-care? There is no harder or more rewarding job than to be the one someone calls Mom. And taking time to care for yourself not only gives you necessary nourishment but it sets an example for your children that self-care and time with God should be prioritized.

These daily devotions are set up to remind you that you're not alone. Each day you'll read a Scripture verse, a devotional, and prayer. Use the ruled lines however you'd like—write down prayers, reflect and write down what's on your mind, make a list of goals, create affirmations, or simply journal about your feelings.

God desires our hearts. He knows what burdens us and gives us joy. But sometimes we are not able to discern this ourselves unless we put our thoughts to paper. May this devotional be a partial record of your current season of life that you can return to in the days and years to come, seeking reminders of the joys and obstacles you once faced. May you come back to these devotions, and your thoughts on them, and treasure them in your heart (Luke 2:51). And, dear friend, beloved daughter of God, may "the LORD turn his face toward you and give you peace" (Numbers 6:26).

For everything there is a season, and a time
for every matter under heaven.
ECCLESIASTES 3:1 ESV

Being a stay-at-home mom is a precious season of life filled with different stages. From babies to toddlers to school-aged kids, then to the tween and teen years, we're never in one stage of motherhood for too long.

Within this blessed season of watching our children grow and develop, we can experience fluctuating periods of joy and grief, blessing and sorrow. What season are you in right now? Are you enjoying a summer of delight? Or maybe you're in a season of winter when the icy winds cut, storms buffet and bruise, and your soul is exposed and vulnerable, like the bare limbs of a tree. Or are you at last entering a season of spring after that long, hard winter? The air may feel chilly, but tender sprouts of hope are unfolding from the ground.

If you are in a difficult season, take heart. Seasons change. You may not be able to change the weather or your circumstances, but you can protect yourself from the elements with prayer and Scripture and by surrounding yourself with people who love you. Take comfort that the Lord is with us through all seasons, whether joyous or challenging.

....

Lord, help me embrace this season of motherhood. Help me embrace the
growth from hard lessons and celebrate the joys, large and small.

....

....

....

....

....

....

....

....

....

....

....

....

....

....

....

....

....

....

....

....

*The LORD appeared to us in the past, saying: "I
have loved you with an everlasting love; I have
drawn you with unfailing kindness."*

JEREMIAH 31:3

Eight billion people live on this planet. Billions more have lived before us. But there has never been anyone exactly like you. You have a personality, a set of gifts, talents, and weaknesses all your own. You have a body size and shape, freckles, wrinkles, a nose, and eyes that set you apart from anyone who has ever lived.

You have a story that is unlike any other story. You've suffered; you have overcome. You've succeeded, and you have failed. You've been hurt, and you have hurt others. You are the hero of your story and sometimes the villain. No one has lived the life you've lived.

No one has ever raised your children. You are a unique parent, shaping and nurturing unique children as only you can.

You are loved. You, personally. You, with all your habits—good and bad—with all your quirky traits and likes and dislikes. You. You are loved deeply and without reservation. If you had never lived, the world would be the worse for it. You matter.

....

*God, thank You for creating me and loving me just as I am. Help me walk
more like Jesus as I embrace who I am.*

....

....

....

....

....

....

....

....

....

....

....

....

....

....

....

....

....

....

....

....

*Jesus replied: "Love the Lord your God with all your
heart and with all your soul and with all your mind."*

MATTHEW 22:37

S taying home with our children is a joyful job, but let's be honest: it's not always easy. Growing and nurturing entire humans, teaching them to honor God, making sure they stay safe and well, ensuring they know they're loved and cared for while thoughtfully disciplining them—well, it's a lot. Especially if you're in the midst of a difficult financial season or dealing with extra health challenges or some other external stressor.

The key to doing it all . . . is realizing we can't. We can't parent perfectly, make zero mistakes, and never let our kids down. And that's okay. We are not commanded to be perfect people, perfect moms, perfect women. Instead, when asked what the greatest commandment was, Jesus replied with the above: love the Lord your God with all your heart and with all your soul and with all your mind.

When we put our focus on our love for God and all our parenting flows from that center point, we are doing what's asked of us. Even if we don't do it perfectly. Even if we fail sometimes. When Jesus is the focus of our lives, our parenting, and all our endeavors, our performances aren't the point. Honoring Him is.

*Jesus, thank You for meeting me in our weak spaces and helping me parent
my children with my love for You at the center.*

....

....

....

....

....

....

....

....

....

....

....

....

....

....

....

....

....

....

Tremble and do not sin; when you are on your
beds, search your hearts and be silent.

PSALM 4:4

If you have small children at home, embracing silence can seem like a far-off dream. *If only*, we think. *If only I had some silence in my day, I would totally cherish it!*

But in practice, when we do get those moments of silence—even if they only come at nap time or bedtime or during showers—instead of cherishing the silence, we often rush to fill it with something. A TV show, some music, an audiobook, a podcast, a phone call. None of these things are bad, of course, but if we find ourselves unable to sit with silence, it begs the question why. Are we afraid to be alone with our thoughts? Or are we concerned about allowing some pending tasks to remain undone as we breathe in the stillness?

Quietness can be scary. Filling the void comes naturally in our modern world that's constantly in motion, constantly filled with static. But what if we welcomed silence as a place of rest? Practice sitting in silence and stillness with the Lord today. Don't mute your worries or fears with white noise. Pray through whatever difficult thoughts may arise in your quiet times, and welcome the peace that silence can bring.

....

Lord Jesus, thank You for the gift of silence. Help me appreciate moments of stillness rather than turn away from them.

But my eyes are fixed on you, Sovereign LORD.
PSALM 141:8

When you're driving, you don't just look forward. You also look back. You lift your head to look into the rearview mirror. You shift your eyes back and forth to the side mirrors. You twist your head to look for blind spots. This helps you when changing lanes, and it helps you in adjusting your speed to remain at a safe distance from other cars. You might even glance into the back seat to make sure the kids are okay, and this ensures your passengers are safe and comfortable.

But what would happen if you spent more time looking backward than forward? What if your glance into the back seat turned into a minute-long distraction? You might, by some chance, make it a little way. But pretty quickly, you'd crash.

Too often, our attention is stuck on the rearview mirror. The objects from our past, while they appear to be years behind, have a much closer hold on our hearts and minds than we realize. Looking back is necessary for moving forward. Just remember to spend far more time looking in the direction you're heading.

....

Father, my past made me who I am today—even the hard parts. But help me to focus on where You want me to go next.

....

....

....

....

....

....

....

....

....

....

....

....

....

....

....

....

....

....

Day 6

Bear with each other and forgive one another if any of you has a grievance against someone. Forgive as the Lord forgave you.

COLOSSIANS 3:13

Nothing prompts unsolicited opinions quite like becoming a mother. Much of this comes from a place of love. Other times, opinions are expressed in the form of judgment, and it can be hurtful or downright offensive.

When others hurt us, sometimes our instinct is to vent about it. But Scripture offers better solutions, and research is beginning to catch up. Scripture encourages healthy conflict resolution (Matthew 18:15–17) and practicing forgiveness. If someone offends you, do you have the grace to turn the other cheek? When unsolicited opinions cause friction in your relationships, do you seek a solution—or someone to rant to? Certainly, there are times when you need to confront, speak truth into others' lives, or gently educate them on their wrongdoings. Other times, you simply need to give grace.

The next time you feel your temper rise or your frustration level increase, ask yourself if this is an opportunity for grace. Our Lord gives us grace upon grace; when you offer it to others, you bless them and protect yourself from engaging in unhealthy coping mechanisms.

....

Lord, thank You for Your gracious nature. Please help me discern when to lovingly confront others and when to graciously let go of offense.

Then Hannah prayed and said: "My heart rejoices in the LORD; in the LORD my horn is lifted high. My mouth boasts over my enemies, for I delight in your deliverance."

I SAMUEL 2:1

You've prayed for years. The second baby you've been hoping for hasn't come. The health situation plaguing you hasn't resolved. The unsustainable financial situation hasn't been relieved. Your unsaved friend still hasn't met the Lord. We all have prayers that seemingly go unanswered, and sometimes we wonder, *Is the Lord even listening*?

Yes, the Lord is listening. Always. But His timing and plan are not always the same as ours. It's a difficult truth to accept, especially when you're praying for something good, something with eternal consequences. How, then, do we find peace in the midst of unanswered prayers?

There are no easy answers, but remember this truth: the same Jesus who gave His life for you, the same God who sent His Son to die for you, the same Holy Spirit who intercedes for you—hears your prayers. If God's love is so vast, deep, and wide, surely His plans for us are also good. Trust in the goodness of God and His plan, and find peace in the fact that God's got you.

....

Lord, it's so hard when prayers seem to go unanswered. Help me trust in Your love and Your plan.

Day 8

Morning by morning he dispenses his justice,
and every new day he does not fail.

ZEPHANIAH 3:5

Our mornings often set the tone for our days. If you wake up to a vomiting toddler, a sleepy teen who misses the bus, an elementary-schooler who suddenly remembers he forgot to do all his homework, that chaos can easily be carried throughout the rest of the day, making it difficult to find your footing.

But consider this type of morning instead: You wake up before anyone else and sit with a cup of coffee or tea. You reflect on the Lord's goodness in your week, and you listen as He speaks to your heart. You have some time to dive into Scripture or read a devotion. And your day begins in a centered, peaceful manner with the Lord as your first focus.

That kind of slow, still morning is possible, but it requires a bit of sacrifice. It may mean extra planning the night before, an earlier bedtime, and an early alarm. But starting the day by putting your expectations, worries, and plans in the Lord's hands is the most restful way to begin. We can't plan every aspect of our days—motherhood teaches us to expect the unexpected—but we can put in the effort to set the tone we want for our mornings.

....

God, thank You for a fresh, new morning each day! Please help me to set a calm, peaceful tone for my busy days.

....

....

....

....

....

....

....

....

....

....

....

....

....

....

....

....

....

....

"Truly I tell you, unless you change and become like little children, you will never enter the kingdom of heaven."

MATTHEW 18:3

It was the world of your childhood. The street on which you lived wasn't a street; it was a frontier to be explored. The playground equipment at the park was a pirate ship, and you were the captain. The woods nearby were full of strange creatures and thrilling unknowns. Most everything you saw in the world was beyond you, which was both a fearful and wonderful thing. Do you see this perspective in your children now?

But then you grew up and were told that being an adult means having all the answers, understanding everything you see, and managing all your responsibilities and relationships with precision. Sometimes when we know in our hearts that such a life is impossible, we retreat into the safety of the superficial, the mundane, the expected.

But your childhood heart understood it: the world is full of possibilities and curiosities, adventures and quests. If you need a reminder, look at your kids and watch how the playground equipment is a castle and they are the royalty. The swing set isn't just for swinging—it's for flying. Play with them. See the world through their eyes. Rediscover your sense of wonder.

....

Jesus, You loved little children. Help me recapture my sense of childlike wonder in this life.

....

....

....

....

....

....

....

....

....

....

....

....

....

....

....

....

....

....

When the hour came, Jesus and his apostles reclined at the table.
LUKE 22:14

What are mealtimes like at your house? Are they loud and chaotic? Are they peaceful and relaxing? Are you sitting around a table, in front of the TV, or on the go as you eat? Maybe it depends on the day.

When the Bible mentions Jesus eating, He is usually seen reclining, as was the Roman custom at the time. Even when eating with His adversaries, the Pharisees, the Bible tells us He reclined (Luke 7:36). And when it was time for the Last Supper, Jesus gathered His closest friends, the disciples, into a room, and they reclined for the meal. Meals were not rushed or scrambling or eaten while working. Instead, mealtimes were opportunities for fellowship and rejuvenation.

Modern moms lead very busy lives, and we don't always have control over how every meal will look. But, as often as you're able, see if you can intentionally turn mealtime into a moment of family fellowship. Meals are opportunities to strengthen our ties with our children, and studies show family meals help kids develop language and social skills. Family meals are linked to improved mental health, healthier eating habits—and even improved academic performance!

....

Jesus, help me see mealtimes as opportunities to nourish my body, soul, and family relationships.

....

....

....

....

....

....

....

....

....

....

....

....

....

....

....

....

....

....

Day 11

*The women who had been companions of Jesus from Galilee
followed along. They saw the tomb where Jesus' body was
placed. Then they went back to prepare burial spices and
perfumes. They rested quietly on the Sabbath, as commanded.*

LUKE 23:55–56 MSG

The work we do as stay-at-home moms is important. Really important. We're growing and raising entire human beings. Their formative years at home will shape so much about who they are and what their futures look like.

In the midst of that important work, it's easy to push rest and self-care to the side. It's easy to prioritize our needs last—or overlook them completely. How many moms do you know who are frazzled, burned out, exhausted, stressed to the point of breaking? Maybe you count yourself among them.

Every parent goes through difficult seasons that stretch us beyond the norm, but if we always feel maxed to our breaking points, that might be a signal we haven't made enough time for self-care. Prioritizing time spent caring for our own souls, minds, and bodies will help us be our best selves for our kids. It's not about being selfish. It's about ensuring our children's needs are met by ensuring their mothers are well cared for too.

....

Lord, please help me prioritize self-care in a way that honors You and honors my family—help me be the best mother I can possibly be.

....

....

....

....

....

....

....

....

....

....

....

....

....

....

....

....

....

....

....

Day 12

*"For my thoughts are not your thoughts, neither
are your ways my ways," declares the LORD.*

ISAIAH 55:8

One of the most terrifying things about raising children in this world is the fear they will be led astray by ungodly ideas. In this information age where it is increasingly difficult to filter everything our children—and especially our teens—consume, sometimes it feels like a giant plastic bubble is the only way to protect them. An internet-free bubble, that is.

The truth of the matter is, while external influences are a valid concern, Scripture says even our own ideas and thoughts are not the same as the Lord's. As much as we want to protect our children from external threats, have we recognized the threat from within?

This isn't as scary as it sounds—it's actually freeing. In having the humility to recognize we don't have it all figured out, that we're capable of error, it prompts us to release that tight-fisted, fear-based control of our children. To teach them to rely on the Lord instead of man—or even mom. God is perfect—we are not. And that truth sets us free to turn our children's hearts over to the Lord.

Father, raising children can be scary sometimes. Help me instill a love of You and Your Word into my children, and help me release fear about their futures.

....

....

....

....

....

....

....

....

....

....

....

....

....

....

....

....

....

....

....

....

....

....

Why, my soul, are you downcast? Why so disturbed within me? Put your hope in God, for I will yet praise him, my Savior and my God.

PSALM 42:5

Does your plate—as a mom, a wife, a woman, a follower of Christ—ever feel overwhelmingly full? Do you sometimes have a particular problem, whether family difficulties, financial hardships, health crises, or something else that feels unbearable? In John 16:33, Jesus told His followers, "I have told you these things, so that in me you may have peace. In this world you will have trouble. But take heart! I have overcome the world." If you're in a time of trouble, take heart; Jesus is not surprised by it. He is not thwarted by it. He is not overcome by it.

If your heart is downcast and your burden feels heavy, Jesus wants you to do something radical: He wants you to give your burden to Him. He wants to take it from you so that you are no longer beaten down or afraid, overwhelmed or bone-weary.

Jesus wants you to have joy during the sunny times of your life, and He also wants to give you peace when you're walking through the storms. In Christ alone our hope is found—fall into His waiting arms. He can—and will—give rest to your soul.

Father, thank You for the refuge from storms available to me in Your strong arms!

And we know that in all things God works for the good of those
who love him, who have been called according to his purpose.

ROMANS 8:28

Hope is a good and necessary thing. Expectation and anticipation help get us through difficult days. But life has a tendency to threaten to squash our hopes and sink our expectations. Maybe you thought becoming a mother would fulfill of all your hopes and dreams, but perhaps the reality has been more difficult. Is this a time of disappointment or a time when your dreams are coming true?

Whether your days are filled with hopeful excitement, dashed dreams, or somewhere in between, take comfort in this fact: God knows where you came from, and He knows where you are going. He knows your past and your future. He knows your every hope and dream. Rather than hoping for and expecting great things of your life, why not hope for and expect great things of your great God? Have peace in the assurance that His plans are always good.

....

Thank You for always coming through, Father, even when Your plans don't match up with my own.

Do not be anxious about anything, but in every situation, by prayer and petition, with thanksgiving, present your requests to God.

PHILIPPIANS 4:6

Of all the life events that might spark fresh anxiety, becoming a parent has to be at the top of the list. There are so many new things to be aware of, so many different dangers and concerns, so much worry about what the future might hold for these precious babies.

But the best news of all is we have an all-powerful God on the throne of our lives and our children's lives. And He tells us to bring every request to him. Maybe you've got a giant request—healing for a sick child, help for a broken marriage, miraculous financial provision. Maybe your requests are smaller—patience to get through the day with a defiant toddler, resolve to break a bad habit, or wisdom in choosing between several good options. Whatever your requests are, big or small, lay them before God.

Sometimes it feels strange to pray about even our biggest problems, as they pale in comparison to the world's great problems. But nothing is too small for the Lord. Scripture says to bring every situation to Him. Your heavenly Father is ready to listen.

Dear Lord, help me remember that nothing is too big or too small to bring to You in prayer.

....

....

....

....

....

....

....

....

....

....

....

....

....

....

....

....

....

....

However, I consider my life worth nothing to me; my only aim is to finish the race and complete the task the Lord Jesus has given me—the task of testifying to the good news of God's grace.

ACTS 20:24

Life is full of beautiful things: vibrant sunflowers, a perfect plate of food, sunsets, bluebirds, and birch trees. And sometimes, it's tempting to show others only the beautiful things in our lives. To present the perfect Instagram version of ourselves, we push the clutter out of the way, catch our best angles, apply a shiny filter, and pen a gushy caption about all that is perfect and right in our worlds. We don't want others to know about the messy parts.

But within the messiness lies our whole truth—our authenticity and vulnerability. Yes, life is beautiful, but it's also complicated. Each of us have our own messes. Sketchy pasts, present struggles, areas in our lives where we have a lot of room to grow. But here's the good news: You don't have to have it all together. And you don't have to hide your messiness from God or others. Sanctification is about the growth of something messy (us) toward something beautiful (Christlikeness). That journey is worth taking out in the open, alongside others on the same journey.

···

Father, thank You for sending Jesus to turn my messy, sinful self into something beautiful. Thank You for loving me, despite my broken bits.

....

....

....

....

....

....

....

....

....

....

....

....

....

....

....

....

....

....

Grace and peace to you from God our
Father and the Lord Jesus Christ.
I Corinthians 1:3

As a stay-at-home mom, it's easy to feel like your time to your-self is being consumed by others. Taking care of your needs, remembering what you do that brings you joy and isn't tied to your children, taking the appropriate amount of time for rest—all of these, and more, can feel completely out of reach for us.

But have you ever considered that you may be the one withhold-ing rest and self-care time from yourself? It's shockingly easy to do. Between the demands of our kids, our partners, our households, life is busy. A lot rests on your shoulders. Do you feel like if you step away, everything will come crashing down?

If you answered an emphatic yes to that question, take heart. You don't have to carry it all, and you don't have to carry it alone. Trust in the One who is holding out His hands to you. Let God shoulder your anxieties. Then see if you can get creative about carving out time for yourself. Is your spouse able to take on the kid duties for a particular time each week? Or can you plan your evenings or mornings around some self-care while the kids are sleeping? You have permission to set it all down for a moment, friend.

....

Lord, show me when I'm unintentionally withholding rest from myself, and teach me to rely on You and others to support me when I'm weary.

But I have calmed and quieted myself, I am like a weaned child with its mother; like a weaned child I am content.

PSALM 131:2

Kids—especially very young ones—don't have much power. Their bodies are tiny and vulnerable. They need protection and reassurance. They're often afraid of the unknown. If you've ever sat with a sick child in a doctor's office, comforted a little one awakened by a nightmare, or walked alongside your child through truly daunting circumstances, like the death of a loved one, you know this well.

When it comes to our troubles, we're often no different from children. In our proud moments, we like to think we can handle every obstacle, but we just can't. We are raising children, yes, but no matter how old we get, we are still God's children, in desperate need of Him. Understanding this is a path to true, lasting peace. As much as you're a helpless child, God is the loving Parent you may have never had.

When you come to Him crying over a scraped knee, He doesn't lecture you to be more careful. Instead He lifts you on His knee like a tender father. He wipes away your tears, kisses your forehead, and tells you it's all going to be okay. When anxiety suffocates your spirit, use it as an opportunity to climb into the lap of the One who will hold you and keep you safe.

....

Father, thank You for caring for me, Your child, as I take care of my children. Help me embrace childlike trust and dependence on You.

Day 19

But the seventh day is a sabbath to the LORD your God.
On it you shall not do any work, neither you, nor your son
or daughter, nor your male or female servant, nor your
animals, nor any foreigner residing in your towns.

EXODUS 20:10

What does your Sabbath normally look like? For many moms, the Sabbath is just like any other day, filled with feeding and caring for our families, sometimes made all the more complicated by friend and family events, errands to be run, and the presence of children home from school. God gave us a Sabbath not because He needed a day to rest but because we need a day to rest, reflect, and refuel. Yes, it's traditionally on Sunday, but if that isn't possible for you, any day of the week works. The principle is what's most important—we need a day to recharge and reset.

Many of our families' needs don't take a day off. But think about ways you can take a day each week to step outside of your usual hustle. Can you prep meals ahead, ensure your errands and chores are completed on other days, and be mindful about scheduling anything on your Sabbath? Make space for a day to let your soul breathe. Take time to let your heart sing of God's goodness in the week past and the week to come.

....

Lord, help me prioritize a Sabbath for my heart, mind, and body. Thank You for showing us how important it is to recharge.

Day 20

I have been crucified with Christ and I no longer live, but
Christ lives in me. The life I now live in the body, I live by faith
in the Son of God, who loved me and gave himself for me.

GALATIANS 2:20

When the Lord gave us the Ten Commandments and included "You shall not covet" (Exodus 20:17 NKJV), He knew that we, as humans, were likely to fall into the trap of comparison and jealousy. It is incredibly easy to do—and at times, it feels harmless. But it robs us of gratitude for what we do have. Particularly for moms, it's easy to compare physical appearances, possessions, personalities, talents, and even spiritual lives. It's easy to compare our children's achievements or gifts, and it's easy to compare parenting styles and lifestyle differences. Comparison is a mind game, and we need to stop playing it.

Do you want freedom from the comparison trap? Try focusing on what you have rather than what you wish you had. Make a list of all you're thankful for. Sure, it seems basic, but it's practically foolproof. When your blessings are written out, right there in front of you, they're much more tangible, and you'll begin to see that you truly are blessed. We all are.

Take the first step in banishing comparison and discontent by beginning that list. You'll be amazed at how long it quickly becomes.

Lord, thank You for my many blessings—including and especially my children and the life You've given me as a stay-at-home mom.

*Finally, brothers and sisters, whatever is true, whatever
is noble, whatever is right, whatever is pure, whatever is
lovely, whatever is admirable—if anything is excellent
or praiseworthy—think about such things.*

PHILIPPIANS 4:8

Anger. Jealousy. Contempt. Annoyance. Shame. How often do you think negatively? If you're stuck in the drop-off line at your child's school, is your mind full of frustration toward other parents? When your spouse disagrees with a decision you made, do you let bitterness overtake you? Do you often find yourself thinking more negatively than positively throughout the day? If so, then perhaps it's time to change the way you think.

It's easy—all too easy—to wallow in self-pity or to fixate on your own anger or someone else's issues. But in doing so, you rob yourself of the joy found in all that is true, noble, right, pure, lovely, admirable, excellent, and praiseworthy. If your mind is a swirling realm of destructive thoughts, there's no room for anything else.

Today, focus instead on what is true—that you are blessed by a God who loves you. Focus on what is praiseworthy—that we are each a work in progress, wrapped in the grace and love of God. Give your mind and body a break from negativity, and rest in the goodness of God.

....

Father, please guide my thoughts and my attitude in a way that glorifies You.

....

....

....

....

....

....

....

....

....

....

....

....

....

....

....

....

....

....

You know the message God sent to the people of Israel, announcing the good news of peace through Jesus Christ, who is Lord of all.

ACTS 10:36

The story of Jesus and His disciples caught out at sea in a storm is well known (Mark 4:35–41). But have you ever thought of applying that story to your own life as a mom? Most often, we focus on Jesus' power in that story—how His simple words calmed a deadly storm. But notice what happened before He spoke: the disciples went to Jesus.

The disciples were on a boat, caught in a horrendous storm. It was a matter of life or death. So what did they do? They turned to Jesus. Was their faith perfect? Not even close. Were they afraid? Yes. Did they doubt Him? Yes. But still they went to Him—and Jesus saved them.

Friend, are you hurrying to Jesus when you're caught in the middle of a parenting storm—or any storm? There's no safer place. Believe in His power and strength. Trust in His goodness and love. He won't let you drown.

....

Father, may I trust in You—especially when the storms in my life are threatening.

Be very careful, then, how you live—not as unwise but as wise,
making the most of every opportunity, because the days are evil.

EPHESIANS 5:15–16

You tell yourself you'll do it later. Someday you'll learn to sew, catch up with an old friend, begin that project, take your mom to lunch, do that special activity with your kids, or plan a date with your spouse. Someday. You'll do it when you have more time and when it's more convenient. Maybe when the kids are older. But why wait for someday? Why not do it today?

When work and chores and responsibilities crowd your life, a certain type of fulfillment can come from doing the special things, the meaningful things. It's not irresponsible to take time away from the everyday to indulge your creative side, to nurture that relationship, or even to just plan and dream a little. These are the moments you'll most remember, and they're the ones—years from now—for which you'll be most grateful. So call your mom; take your dad to the game; reunite with an old friend; learn to bake. Plan that special time with your kids. Finally take that family staycation. Seek out the moments that really matter.

Lord, help me make time for special memories. Help me nurture the relationships that matter most.

But I will sing of your strength, in the
morning I will sing of your love.

PSALM 59:16

Morning. It's the time to get up, get ready, and begin your day. It's the starting point of the day. And it's also a wonderful time to rest. Yes, you did just wake up, and yes, you have a million things to do. Get the kids up, get them fed, get them to school. Feed the dogs. Clean the kitchen. Prepare for the rest of your chores and errands for the day. But if you begin your day with a peaceful spirit, the remainder of your day is more likely to be calm too.

Savor the morning. Take a moment to slowly breathe in and out. Yawn and stretch and open the curtains. Enjoy the sunrise. Sit with your Bible and your coffee and find respite and relief in the promises of your Lord. Let your mind be filled with joy for the day. Before the demands begin, cars are started, traffic is jammed, and patience is running thin, enjoy these quiet moments of the morning. Again, it might require the sacrifice of getting up a little earlier to make it happen, but try it out. See how it affects the rest of your day.

....

Lord, let the quiet beauty of my morning carry me through the day.

*Let us then approach God's throne of grace with
confidence, so that we may receive mercy and
find grace to help us in our time of need.*

HEBREWS 4:16

With today's technology, it's easier than ever to stay connected with friends, family, current events, and even former classmates. Just a few clicks and swipes and relationships are easily established, nourished, and renewed.

But connecting with Jesus is even easier. There's no technology required, because He's only a simple prayer away. No cell service? No problem. You can connect with Jesus even in the middle of nowhere, or in the dead of night, or in the middle of the afternoon. He never ignores your messages, and He never asks if He can get back with you later. God is available anytime and all the time.

Isn't that a relief? Isn't that an amazing promise? Jesus is there for you always, no matter the time or circumstance. He can give you the counsel, encouragement, and peace you so desperately need. Connect with Jesus today; He's only a prayer away.

....

Dear Jesus, thank You for never being too busy, tired, or overwhelmed to hear my prayers.

....

....

....

....

....

....

....

....

....

....

....

....

....

....

....

....

....

....

He stilled the storm to a whisper; the waves of the
sea were hushed. They were glad when it grew calm,
and he guided them to their desired haven.

PSALM 107:29–30

When you think of the word *retreat*, you probably don't think of your own home with its piles of laundry, the mile-long to-do list, and the cluttered countertops. Instead, visions of white, sandy beaches or rustic mountain cabins probably fill your thoughts. After all, a retreat should be a break away from the demands of ordinary, everyday life, right?

Often, we don't have the time or money to go on a faraway retreat. Coordinating childcare can be a logistical hurdle. And perhaps when we can get away, we choose to spend that time with our spouse instead of prioritizing a personal retreat. So have you ever thought of letting your home be your destination for retreat?

Even if you simply designate one spot to be your haven, it can be made into a mini sanctuary. Clear away the clutter and banish distractions. Add a candle, a painting, green plants, or your favorite chair. And then . . . retreat. Take a nap, read your Bible, and revel in your haven. Allow yourself to fully retreat—for a moment, for an hour, for an afternoon. Whatever time is available to you, grab it. And enjoy!

....

Heavenly Father, please bless me with extraordinary rest in my ordinary
haven.

You are my strength, I sing praise to you; you, God,
are my fortress, my God on whom I can rely.
PSALM 59:17

Have you ever met a mom who had an unbelievably crazy-busy schedule—kids in every sport, after-school dance and music lessons, commitments at church, maybe even a job on top of it all—but instead of being stressed and fatigued, that mom exuded a peaceful calm and an utter reliance on Jesus? That's called *inner rest*. It's a peace that depends not upon circumstances, personality, or even organization; instead, it comes from a prayerful spirit and an intentional dependence on the Lord.

With inner rest, your life may look hectic on the outside, and you may not get as much sleep as you wish each night, but your daily, hourly, and sometimes minute-by-minute surrendering to the Lord keeps your spirit firmly planted in peace instead of despair.

Dear friend, do you need to focus on internal rest today? Whether our schedules look crazy-busy or less intense, we all need this type of inner peace. It's available to you. Ask the Lord to lead you to true, deep inner rest, to the peace and calm that can only come from Him. Ask, and He will meet you in your need.

....

God, I deeply desire inner peace. Please help me surrender my life completely to You, relying on Your strength rather than my own.

....
....
....
....
....
....
....
....
....
....
....
....
....
....
....
....
....
....
....
....
....

And so we know and rely on the love God has for us. God is
love. Whoever lives in love lives in God, and God in them.
I John 4:16

Have you ever been on the receiving end of unfair judgment about your parenting? Has your journey as a mom been blessedly free of hurtful words and difficult conflict, or has it been plagued by these things?

If you've experienced difficulties, you're not alone. And some of those hurts run deep. We may still feel the pain, even if it happened years ago. A harsh comment, broken trust, a stab in the back—we have all experienced some sort of hurt in our lives, and it can be particularly painful when it involves our children or our identities as mothers. But if that hurt has calcified into bitterness, or if you're still holding on to pain, shame, or a desire for revenge, it's time to let go.

First John 4:16 reminds us of how we are to live even amid the hurts and sorrows of this world: we are to live in love. Notice that God's Word doesn't say we are to live in love unless we've been hurt. No, we are to live in love, period.

As this truth sinks in, ask your Savior to show you how to let go of past hurts. Beseech Him to replace them with His love, joy, peace, kindness, and hope. Christ can heal even the deepest wound and free your heart and mind from the effects of painful words.

···

Help me live in love, dear Jesus, especially when I've been wronged.

....

....

....

....

....

....

....

....

....

....

....

....

....

....

....

....

....

....

....

As you do not know the path of the wind, or how the
body is formed in a mother's womb, so you cannot
understand the work of God, the Maker of all things.
ECCLESIASTES 11:5

A s children, we have big dreams for the future. As we grow up, enter high school, go to college or get a job, get married, have children, and watch the years pass by, our lives can branch out in countless directions. Some of those childhood dreams come true, but others do not.

Does your life look completely different than you thought it would? Did you always dream of having children and staying home to raise them, or is this a detour in the original plan? Perhaps your list of dreams included motherhood, but now you're watching that important role overtake all other dreams you'd hoped for. Life is hard—especially when hopes are deferred and dreams don't come true.

If you feel this way, look to the Lord. He understands your frustrations and disappointments. And more than anything, He wants you to confide in Him and trust Him to lead you. God can transform those dashed hopes into part of His amazing plan—and you can rest in fulfilling His purpose for your life—whatever that may be, and however motherhood fits into it.

Oh, Lord my God, I place my hopes and dreams in Your steady and loving hands.

....

....

....

....

....

....

....

....

....

....

....

....

....

....

....

....

....

Whatever your hand finds to do, do it with all your might.

ECCLESIASTES 9:10

If you had a week to do absolutely anything you love, what would it include? Maybe you love games and puzzles. Maybe you love to work in your garden or focus on sports or fitness. Maybe you like hiking, reading, spending time with friends, or spending time alone. Maybe baking makes you smile.

These are things that give you life. They're not the mundane "I have time so I might as well clean out the garage" activities (though that does bring joy to some—not judging). These are the things that not only bring you joy but also leave you feeling refreshed and fulfilled.

Incorporate one of your favorite activities into your week. Maybe you can't go adventuring on hiking trails for a whole week, but how about an afternoon? Browse through a gardening magazine at lunch or bake some cookies after you pick up the kids from school. Giving yourself even small doses of these life-giving activities will enrich your daily life full of important must-do activities.

....

Lord, show me ways to incorporate the things I love into my everyday life.

Who is wise? Let them realize these things. Who
is discerning? Let them understand.

HOSEA 14:9

An energy drink or a cup of coffee will give you a surge of alertness and drive to conquer the world. That may last a few hours. After that, your body is back to its tired, passive state. If you need to be up again, you'll need another dose. Water isn't as exciting. It's flavorless, and although you may feel better after a glass, it doesn't provide the same effect as the energy drink.

But water is real. That's what your body really needs. Water will truly satisfy your thirst, and, coupled with other healthy habits, drinking enough water each day will give you energy that can last years, not just a few fleeting hours.

As it is with beverages, so it is with many of our spiritual and emotional needs. There are many supposed quick fixes out there, but what we actually need is deep, satisfying, real nourishment to our souls. How do you spot what's real? It's often sourced in creation and made by our Creator. It isn't as attractive or quick-acting as its counterfeit. But by moving nearer to the source, you'll more readily recognize what's true and real.

....

Father, please help sharpen my discernment to identify what's real and
what honors You most.

....

....

....

....

....

....

....

....

....

....

....

....

....

....

....

....

....

....

....

Let all creation rejoice before the LORD, for he comes,
he comes to judge the earth. He will judge the world in
righteousness and the peoples in his faithfulness.

PSALM 96:13

Kids spend more and more time inside, often in front of a screen, but experts are encouraging parents to take their kids outside. Why? Because being outside in nature helps children not just physically but also mentally and socially. It boosts their intellect, immune systems, and emotional well-being. It's just a good thing to do.

And it's not only good for our kids; it's good for us too. Can you find time today to go outside? Take the kids for a bike ride, or get your heart rate up with a walk. Find a pool to splash in, walk by the lake, or explore a hiking trail. You'll be refreshed in a way that only the majesty of God's creation can provide. The combination of trees, fresh air, sunshine, wind, water, physical movement, the smell of dirt, and the beauty of bright blooms is healing in a unique way that nothing else is. So open the door and step outside to recharge your batteries.

....

God, the beauty of Your world amazes me. Refresh me with Your creation.

Day 33

*The LORD is in his holy temple; let all
the earth be silent before him.*

HABAKKUK 2:20

The life of a mom is rarely quiet. Whether we're caring for babies, teens, or anyone in between, silence can be hard to come by. It's incredibly easy to get caught up in the constant buzz of life as a stay-at-home mom. Sitting in a quiet place almost feels . . . wasteful and decadent. But, dear friend, that's just what you need to do. It's what we all need sometimes.

Turning down the volume on the demands of life, tuning out everything except the voice of your heavenly Father, is crucial. Sitting with Him in the morning, at the end of the day, or anytime you're able to will calm your soul. Just a few moments of silence in His presence will help refocus your eyes and heart on Him instead of on the many demands vying for your attention. Let His voice speak over any troubles you have in your life, and allow the quiet power of His Word to penetrate your life. Intentionally seek silence in your life.

....

Father, help me tune out the noise of the world and focus on You. Help me remember that while my responsibilities are important, taking time to be with You is too.

For to us a child is born, to us a son is given, and the government
will be on his shoulders. And he will be called Wonderful
Counselor, Mighty God, Everlasting Father, Prince of Peace.

ISAIAH 9:6

You think about last night, and you shake your head. There was so much you wanted to get done, but instead you fell asleep on the couch, completely exhausted. And that already-huge to-do list? It only got longer. Tasks to be done around the house. Items the kids need for school. Those volunteer hours you promised the church. Sometimes it feels like it never ends.

Friend, give yourself grace. If you're juggling too many commitments, maybe you need to toss a few to someone else. If you're falling behind in life's demands, you may be expecting too much of yourself. Be gentle, exceedingly gentle, with your tired body and mind.

When Jesus called the weary and heavy laden to Himself, he didn't berate or lecture them. Instead, He welcomed them, and He promised to carry their load (Matthew 11:28). Why not give the Savior your heavy load? Hear His words of love and grace instead of your own words of condemnation. Find rest in the Prince of Peace.

....

Dear loving Savior, please take this heavy load and fill me with peace.

We are hard pressed on every side, but not crushed;
perplexed, but not in despair; persecuted, but not
abandoned; struck down, but not destroyed.
2 CORINTHIANS 4:8–9

Before Jesus left this earth, He said, "In this world you will have trouble. But take heart! I have overcome the world" (John 16:33). Jesus stated a fact: we will have trouble. Life will be hard. Maybe your journey as a mom has been blissfully trouble free so far. But odds are you've hit some hiccups along the way. Whether it's a child who has a disability or behavioral struggles, a marriage that isn't as strong as you'd hoped, or something happening around your family rather than within it, most of us hit speed bumps, roadblocks, and unexpected challenges along our parenting journeys.

If you're feeling as if your life is just one battle after another, that doesn't surprise Jesus. He predicted it for His disciples thousands of years ago, and it's still true for His followers today. But Jesus didn't leave us to sink in that trouble; instead, He gave us hope.

We have hope because through His death and resurrection, He has already overcome the world. We don't need to worry, fear, or despair. We know how the story will end—with Jesus' complete victory!

···

Jesus, in hard times, I cling to You and to Your words of encouragement.
Thank You for being my refuge.

Every athlete exercises self-control in all things. They do it
to receive a perishable wreath, but we an imperishable.
I CORINTHIANS 9:25 ESV

If you've ever watched interviews of Olympic athletes or read an article about their training regimen, you've noticed that they all have something in common, whether they're gymnasts, sprinters, or speed skaters. They all allow their bodies to recover within their training cycles.

God didn't create our bodies to be in continual motion, and sometimes life as a mom makes it feel like continual motion is required. But resting allows the body time to repair its muscles and strengthen itself. That's true if you're an Olympic runner or if you can barely jog around the block.

So . . . have you been giving yourself the space to recover through self-care and plenty of rest? Yes, your life is full of important demands, from cooking and cleaning to raising children, from ministry demands to homeschooling to community commitments, and everything in between. Each of our lives looks a little different, but we have one thing in common. Our lives are demanding, and these demands put stress on our bodies, minds, and spirits. Take a tip from some Olympic athletes: work hard, and then allow yourself space to recover.

....

Father, I push myself too hard sometimes. Help me make space for recovery.

Trust in the LORD with all your heart and lean not
on your own understanding; in all your ways submit
to him, and he will make your paths straight.

PROVERBS 3:5–6

F ew things in life are scarier, more daunting, than the idea of being solely responsible for another's life—let alone the life of a tiny human. Often we don't feel adequate. We aren't patient enough, wise enough, gentle enough. We don't have all the right answers.

It requires true courage to step up to this task. But the very best news is that we don't have to do it on our own strength. Instead, in faith and deep trust, we can release control and surrender the lives of our children to God's plans. Even when we feel weak, still our human tendency is to try to hold on to control—to rely on our own power, our own understanding, our own strength.

But there's freedom, peace, and joy in releasing control and trusting our good, kind, wise God to handle our children's futures better than we ever could. When we surrender to the Lord, we can rest assured our loving Father will take care of us—and our kids.

....

Lord, motherhood can be overwhelming and scary. Please help me trust
that You have a good plan for my kids.

....

....

....

....

....

....

....

....

....

....

....

....

....

....

....

....

....

....

....

....

Don't grumble against one another, brothers and sisters, or
you will be judged. The Judge is standing at the door!
JAMES 5:9

S ometimes complaining feels good, doesn't it? At least for a few
minutes. But then you usually end up feeling even more frustrated,
jaded, or angry than before. Complaining doesn't help you process your
emotions. It doesn't help you forget or move on. It solidifies your feelings
of being wronged. And those feelings can begin to take root deep down
inside you, hardening your heart.

Where there is complaining, there is no peace. Peace comes from
a contented heart, from understanding that life isn't always fair, and
from choosing to embrace what life has to offer you. Peace comes from
healthy conflict resolution and processing our feelings with maturity,
grace, and solid boundaries. Complaining, on the other hand, brings
only weariness.

The next time you find yourself complaining, note how your body
reacts. You may feel your blood pressure rise, shoulders tighten, and
hands curl into fists. This isn't healthy. Let go of your complaints, turn
them over to God in prayer, and let Him replace them with peace and
contentment.

....

Lord, when a grumbling spirit threatens to take over my mind and heart,
please replace it with peaceful trust in You.

....

....

....

....

....

....

....

....

....

....

....

....

....

....

....

....

....

....

....

....

....

You, LORD, hear the desire of the afflicted; you
encourage them, and you listen to their cry.

PSALM 10:17

Y ou look at the calendar, and your heart sinks. Every night of
the week is busy, and the weekend is crammed with activities,
chores, and errands. Add something extra into the mix—a child really
struggling in school, a health crash, a relationship catastrophe—and
you may find yourself quickly swamped.

We all can relate. Overscheduling is easy to do, and it's hard to
know how to maintain a less hectic agenda, even without any "extras"
to swamp us. After all, your family needs you, the church needs you,
your friends need you—and after saying yes to all their needs, there's
little, if any, time left for you. Sound relatable?

It's true that we all have commitments we can't bail on, and some
seasons of life are busier than others. When you're overwhelmed with
overscheduling, turn to God. Give Him your schedule. Ask Him to help
you sift through your calendar and reveal to you the things that can
go and the things that should stay. Lean on Him and His strength. He
will uphold you, He will help you, He will guide you to a more peaceful "normal," and He will be your anchor in times of hardship that
threaten to overwhelm you.

....

Lord, show me the activities I can let go of and guide me to those things I
should keep.

....

....

....

....

....

....

....

....

....

....

....

....

....

....

....

....

....

....

....

Carry each other's burdens, and in this way
you will fulfill the law of Christ.

GALATIANS 6:2

*H*ow is your mom network looking these days? Do you have friends who are on this journey with you? Even if you don't have many fellow moms in your life, maybe you have close friends who support you as a person and as a parent. It's really important.

We all need a helping hand sometimes. Being a mother comes with many joys, but it's also a lot of work, and again, some seasons are harder than others. Having a supportive network of those who understand you can be a lifesaver. In turn, you are there for them when they need it, offering help, compassion, and community.

If this feels like it's lacking in your life, don't worry. You can always make the choice to build community. Is there a group for moms at your church? If you homeschool, what about a co-op? If your kids are in a traditional school environment, are there groups, clubs, or organizations you can join to grow and nurture your network of parents? How about the family down the street you carpool with? Supporting others can be a powerful testimony for friends and neighbors who don't know Jesus yet.

....

Father, thank You for the precious friends in my life. Please open my eyes to the needs of those around me.

....

....

....

....

....

....

....

....

....

....

....

....

....

....

....

....

....

....

....

....

....

Surely you have granted him unending blessings and
made him glad with the joy of your presence.
PSALM 21:6

Take a moment to think of the many blessings in your life. Perhaps you'll think of things like your beautiful children, health, loving parents, a warm bed, a clean bathroom, a hot shower, a cup of coffee on a dreary day, friends who care, a lovely garden, a godly spouse, a running car—the list could go on and on and on. As you open your eyes to the blessings around you, both small and large, the awareness is life changing. And as you intentionally look for what God has given you, you'll continue to see more and more and still more blessings.

Focusing on gratitude is healthy for everyone, and it's especially important when we're stressed out. It's all too easy to sink into a negative attitude when we're stretched thin. But by intentionally shifting our focus to all God has done, is doing, and will continue to do, we are encouraged to trust in His plan. He has been faithful in the past, and He will continue to be faithful to us now and forever.

....

Lord, help me to see my many blessings as wonderful proof that You keep Your promises.

Day 42

Therefore do not worry about tomorrow, for tomorrow will
worry about itself. Each day has enough trouble of its own.

MATTHEW 6:34

A phrase is added to the Serenity Prayer in many recovery group meetings: *just for today*. It's actually a variation on the longer version of Reinhold Niebuhr's prayer: "living one day at a time, enjoying one moment at a time."

Those prayers can be especially helpful for people struggling with addiction, but you don't have to be dealing with substance abuse for life to feel unmanageable. Facing your problems, surrendering, finding peace within yourself, working for peace with others, and giving control to God are the keys to peace for everyone.

But none of this happens overnight, so even if you're pursuing these strategies, you can still find yourself overwhelmed. God has a job and you have a job. Your main job is to focus on the peace of today—very often, on peace in the next moment. Have the wisdom to know that tomorrow will worry about itself. The time for your peace and serenity is now.

....

God, my life can feel chaotic and worrisome sometimes. Help me find the
peace of the moment and let tomorrow worry about itself.

*"You shall not make for yourself an image in the form of anything
in heaven above or on the earth beneath or in the waters below."*

EXODUS 20:4

A lot of moms feel pressure to present a certain image, especially on social media. We see influencer moms, celebrity moms, even our mom friends who seem always to be put together and polished. And sometimes, we feel a lot of pressure to live up to that image.

If you are trying to keep others impressed with your home, family life, possessions, and even your kids, it's not doing you—or anyone else—any good. And, chances are, you're more than a little tired. It's a lot of work to try to maintain a perfect illusion.

Letting others into the messy, raw, frustrating, and joyful parts of your life is the most authentic thing you can do. And authenticity brings freedom. It bypasses the superficial and allows friendships to grow and respect to deepen. Being honest about both the good and bad in life loosens your hold on that picture-perfect, squeaky-clean—and oh-so-phony—image. Instead, you can simply be yourself—the beautiful you the Lord created.

Are you keeping others locked outside of your real life? Take a chance and let them in. You'll be amazed by the peace and joy that authenticity can bring.

....

Forgive me for wanting others to think my life is perfect, Lord. Help me instead to be open and honest.

Day 44

But according to his promise we are waiting for new
heavens and a new earth in which righteousness dwells.
2 PETER 3:13 ESV

The internet is a massive part of our lives today. It gives us answers—like the location of the nearest coffee shop with at least a 4.5-star rating, or the name of the twenty-second US president. It provides directions, health information, and recipes. And it does it all in less than a second.

But there are questions even the internet cannot answer. Will my children be happy when they grow up? Will we maintain a good relationship? Will we get past this latest financial crisis? Am I making the right educational choice for my kids? The list of unanswerable parenting and life questions seems unending.

Are you wrestling with unanswered questions? Do you wish God would just write the answer in the sky or appear in a burning bush? Talk to Him about it. Tell Him your worries, and confess your fears. Then, ask the Lord to give you peace about these unanswered questions, because, unlike the internet, God cares for you. Embrace that truth, friend. It's freeing and empowering to know God is in control of our lives.

....

Lord, You know my future, and even now You're directing my path. I will
wait on You—help me.

*And which of you by being anxious can add
a single hour to his span of life?*
MATTHEW 6:27 ESV

The days have a tendency to fly by, leaving you out of breath and out of energy. You want to live life with more peace, more intention. You want to have a calmer, less frenzied approach, but you're not sure how to change your situation. If that's you, friend, you are not alone. So many of us struggle with it. Have you ever considered structuring your week so it's more conducive to taking care of yourself?

Make a schedule at the beginning of the week and fill in all of your must-do items. As you list them, ask yourself if any of the items can be shared or altered. Can you figure out a carpool for your kids? Can you share meal preparation with a spouse or a friend? Can you better use the alone time you do have? Can you delegate chores to older kids or hire some things out, if it's in the budget?

After seeing the structure of your week, you may be able to tweak it and allow yourself time for self-care every day. A restful week—one with the right balance of productivity and recharging—won't simply fall into your waiting arms; it takes discipline and planning, but it will be worth it.

....

Lord, help me find a structure for my life that supports my well-being and the well-being of my family.

....

....

....

....

....

....

....

....

....

....

....

....

....

....

....

....

....

....

....

O LORD, you are my God; I will exalt you; I will
praise your name, for you have done wonderful
things, plans formed of old, faithful and sure.

ISAIAH 25:1 ESV

God is writing a story in each of our lives. Some stories are more dramatic than others. Maybe you grew up in a Christian home with two loving parents, or perhaps your parents divorced, leaving you dazed and wounded. Perhaps you endured a difficult childhood, are battling anxiety, or have experienced a radical transformation that brought you to Christ.

Everyone's story is different, and when Jesus is part of it, everyone's story is beautiful. Don't ever feel ashamed of yours. Beloved child of God, the Lord of all creation is the Author of your story, and it is a reflection of His handiwork in your life. Each and every story is one of redemption and beauty.

Your story has the potential to touch other lives—whether it's full of drama or full of peace. Revel in the fact that God is continuing to pen your story, shaping it into a masterpiece. He is actively shaping the stories of your children too. Because Jesus came, we already know the ending of the story. It's a happy one!

....

Lord, help me remember You are the Author holding the pen, writing my story.

Please accept my blessing that is brought to you, because God
has dealt graciously with me, and because I have enough.

GENESIS 33:11 ESV

We live in a materialistic society. One of the easiest lies to believe is this: more stuff will make you happier. It's not a sin to go shopping; to buy a new car, a house, an oven, or a cute outfit. It's not a sin to dress our kids well or buy toys for them. But if you're trying to purchase happiness and contentment, then what you're really buying is the lie.

There is nothing in this world that can perfectly satisfy. You could own a private villa in Italy, have a getaway flat in Central London, drive a Tesla, and buy a new wardrobe for your whole family every season, but without Christ, you'll never be perfectly satisfied. Only Jesus can fill the emptiness in our hearts. Only He provides true contentment and joy. So if you're wondering whether to buy or not to buy, remind yourself that true contentment cannot be purchased. It can be found only in Christ. Only He will satisfy.

....

You are all I truly need, Jesus. Change me until You are all I want.

For all have sinned and fall short of the glory of
God, and are justified by his grace as a gift, through
the redemption that is in Christ Jesus.
ROMANS 3:23–24 ESV

E phesians 2:8 says, "It is by grace you have been saved, through faith—and this is not from yourselves, it is the gift of God." Did you see that, dear reader? You are not saved through your own works. God isn't counting the number of times you do something good, waiting for you to reach a magic number that equals salvation. He isn't looking over your shoulder while you raise your kids, making sure you make zero mistakes, marking you down if you fail. He isn't looking at you to save yourself. Salvation is His gift.

You are saved by grace, and it is only by grace that you can come before the Lord in thanksgiving, sadness, and doubt. It is only because of God's grace that you can have eternal life. It has nothing to do with what you do and everything to do with what Christ did.

Isn't that a life-changing gift? We can stand firm in the salvation of Christ. We do not have to work for God's love—it is already ours. Praise God, for He has done good things for us!

Your grace brings me to my knees and humbles me. Thank You, Lord, thank You!

Those who know your name trust in you, for you,
LORD, have never forsaken those who seek you.

PSALM 9:10

Does your future look blurry? Are you uncertain of the direction your life is taking—or even should take? We all deal with that at one time or another, and it's especially scary when we consider those questions for our children. Where will they go? Who will they be?

But take comfort. God is an expert at bringing blurry futures into perfect focus. He may do it only one step at a time, one moment at a time. But you can trust His vision for your life and your children's lives.

In those times when the future seems blurry and uncertain, turn to God for direction. He promises that He'll never forsake those who seek Him. He will never leave you lost and wandering. Rest in the guidance He will give you, trusting Him day by day, moment by moment, step by step.

If you are a follower of Christ, the Lord is with you always. He won't let you down, and He'll never forget your needs. He loves our children even more than we do—as wild as that is to think about! Take comfort in knowing that the Lord will bring perfect focus to your life when you seek Him.

....

When my future looks blurry, I trust that You're in control and guiding my life, Lord. Please help me make wise choices in line with Your will.

....

....

....

....

....

....

....

....

....

....

....

....

....

....

....

....

....

....

Day 50

I know what it is to be in need, and I know what it is to have plenty. I have learned the secret of being content in any and every situation, whether well fed or hungry, whether living in plenty or in want. I can do all this through him who gives me strength.

PHILIPPIANS 4:12–13

Are you a "glass half-empty" or a "glass half-full" person? Your answer can make all the difference when it comes to cultivating a mindset of contentment. As humans, we naturally bend toward a desire for more, and we think fulfillment will come if only we just had _____. Fill in the blank with whatever—more stuff, a better relationship, children who behaved better, a better job for your spouse. Though we may know that more stuff doesn't equal happiness, it's often a tough truth for our hearts to understand.

When you're feeling discontented, are you focusing on what you don't have? Are you seeing the glass as half-empty? Why not deliberately choose to see your glass as half-full? Living a "half-empty life" is exhausting. It keeps you focused on the disappointments, and it robs you of contentment and joy. Choose to shift your thinking. Look around at your life: God has blessed you richly, even in difficult times. Rest in the Lord's abundant provision—and rejoice as He fills your cup to overflowing.

....

Lord, help me to shift my focus to something that honors You and the current stage of my journey. Help me be content in all circumstances.

The LORD gave them rest on every side.

JOSHUA 21:44

Most people think of rest merely as sleep—it's what you do when you fall into bed and close your eyes. But resting is not just physical; it's also a state of being.

Think about the past week. How busy has it been? Have the kids' schedules been demanding? Maybe it hasn't been very busy, but it's been particularly stressful for one reason or another. Here's a secret: no matter how busy it has or hasn't been, no matter how much stress you're dealing with, you can still adopt a mindset of rest.

Rest is more than sleep and more than simply not working. True rest is being content in the Lord. It's living your life trusting Him and surrendering control over your life to Him. Because when we surrender control to the Lord, when we practice gratitude and contentment in our lives, it helps us put the worries of the day in their proper place. They no longer control us. Instead, our capable, kind, loving Father is the master of our lives.

Physical rest is important, but it's equally important to allow your soul to spiritually rest. Find rest today, even in the midst of busyness and cares. Pass your worries to the Lord and find contentment for the deepest part of your soul.

....

Father God, teach me to rest in all ways—physically, mentally, and spiritually.

For the sake of Christ, then, I am content with
weaknesses, insults, hardships, persecutions, and
calamities. For when I am weak, then I am strong.
2 Corinthians 12:10 esv

No one likes to feel weak or vulnerable—especially in our culture that prides itself on self-sufficiency and independence. We're expected to be super moms, managing our child's physical, spiritual, and emotional needs with ease, while simultaneously maintaining a healthy marriage and an Instagram-worthy home.

But consider this: God's power is made perfect in your weakness. God says it Himself in His Word. The apostle Paul actually boasted of his own weakness, because in his weakness, he rested in the strength of the Lord. Paul's own agenda and desires were set aside, and the Lord was then able to work powerfully in his life.

What does living in weakness look like? It doesn't mean being lazy or neglectful. It doesn't mean being a pushover or letting people harm you. It means fully relying on the Lord's strength rather than your own. Any hardship that comes up is simply handed to the Lord, and in His strength, He handles it.

You are strong when you are weak because that's when God's power is working most greatly through you. Rest from your striving, and believe that the Lord can handle it.

....

Jesus, may I become less so that You become greater.

For you have been my hope, Sovereign LORD,
my confidence since my youth.

PSALM 71:5

We look for joy and fulfillment in many places: a new house, our marriages, children, or a hobby. While these things can certainly bring us happiness, they can't give us the deep, soul-stirring, everlasting joy and contentment we crave. Do you find yourself wanting more from life? Do you feel a yearning you can't quite fill? That's your desire for God.

You can have the nicest clothes, most loving family, or largest social group, but without a deep satisfaction in the Lord, you'll feel empty. You won't feel joyful; you'll feel hollow. Does that resonate with you? Motherhood is an extremely important role, but even that cannot fulfill this longing.

Ask the Lord to fill you with the joy that can only come from Him. Make spending time with Him a priority and converse with Him throughout your day, whatever else is on your to-do list. We all have a longing within us that can only be filled by God, and He's waiting to fill it. He's waiting to give you joy.

....

God, fill this hole in my life with Your presence and Your joy; remind me of the joy I felt when I first met You.

....

....

....

....

....

....

....

....

....

....

....

....

....

....

....

....

....

....

Sing to him, sing praise to him; tell of all his wonderful acts.

1 Chronicles 16:9

If you've ever taken a walk with one of your kids when they were small, you know it's often more stopping than walking. They'll want to look at every bug, crack in the sidewalk, fallen leaf, and budding flower. They'll bend down to inspect a colony of ants and look up to see the airplane roaring overhead. Kids live with their eyes wide-open.

But as we grow into adults, something changes. Pebbles and grass are exchanged for phones and laptop screens. That sense of wonder is replaced with worry and stress. Instead of taking our time, we rush, rush, rush. We don't stop to see the beauty around us. One of the most beautiful things about becoming a parent is the opportunity to see life through the eyes of a child again—if we're aware enough to notice.

Slow down and keep your eyes wide-open. Notice the way your spouse laughs or your dog settles in the sunlight. Breathe in the aroma of fresh bread as you pass the bakery. Savor your cup of coffee. Living with eyes wide-open will invite more wonder into your life—and a more childlike spirit.

....

Father, help me recapture my wonder for Your creation and my life. Help me view the world as I did when I was a child.

But the wisdom that comes from heaven is first of all
pure; then peace-loving, considerate, submissive, full
of mercy and good fruit, impartial and sincere.

JAMES 3:17

*H*elp. It's a short word, but for many, it's so difficult to say. Sometimes especially for moms. We're used to helping others and making sure our families' lives are running smoothly and surely. We may not even notice we need help, or if we do, we feel guilty asking for it. But asking for help isn't about helplessness; asking for help is about honesty, enlisting others, the love of God, and prayer.

Honesty means acknowledging that you are human and you can't do it all. So at times, you need to enlist others, which means actively reaching out for help. It isn't shameful. It's a step toward living a more balanced and sustainable life. And it allows others the freedom to admit that they, too, need help.

You can also enlist God's help, trusting that He will provide it. How can you seek God's assistance? Through prayer. Open your mouth and heart, and spill out all your worries and struggles before the Lord. Seek Him; seek H-E-L-P.

....

Lord, give me the humility, honesty, and courage to reach out for help when
I need it, and give me the compassion and empathy to notice when others
need my help.

....

....

....

....

....

....

....

....

....

....

....

....

....

....

....

....

....

....

....

Everyone was amazed and gave praise to God. They were filled
with awe and said, "We have seen remarkable things today."
LUKE 5:26

How often do you think about the next hour, day, month, or year? How often have you thought, *I can't wait until* . . . ? Do you find yourself wishing today would hurry up and be over so that you can get on with your real life? Have you ever wished this season of parenting would fast-forward to something a little easier, a little less stressful? It's understandable, especially if you're in the midst of potty training, the Fearsome Fours, tween drama, or college planning with your senior. But try to remember: this present day is God's gift to you. Open it up; enjoy it fully.

In this present moment, God gives you breath. He keeps your heart beating. He woke you up this morning, and He reveals Himself to you all throughout the day—through the kindness of a stranger, the color-ful autumn leaves or spring flowers, the beauty of Scripture in your morning reading. Don't be so focused on the future that you miss the present, because it is filled with God's blessings. There is much to be enjoyed in this day. Look for it, and then embrace the gift of this pres-ent moment.

....

Jesus, when I'm wishing time would pass by, remind me that today is a gift
from You.

My soul is in deep anguish. How long, LORD, how long? Turn,
LORD, and deliver me; save me because of your unfailing love.

PSALM 6:3–4

Prayers are mysterious. They flow upward in tears, in words, and in songs. They aren't always fully formed or thought out. And sometimes, the only word we seem to be able to pray is *help*.

Whatever your prayer, if you are coming to the Lord with your whole heart, you can be full of expectation. He is a living God who does mighty and awesome works for His children—and your children. He loves to answer prayer—in small ways, in large ways, in ways that exceed your expectations and even your imagination. Answered prayers aren't luck or merely happy coincidences—they are the God of the universe orchestrating the tiniest details of your life into beautiful blessings.

Think of how much you love your children and how much you enjoy blessing them. Now imagine you always bless them perfectly with exactly what they need. If you're waiting for a prayer to be answered, keep pounding on the door of heaven. And rest in knowing that your prayer will be answered—in the fullness of time, in the wisdom of God, and with His unfailing love.

....

Father, I give You my prayers, and I wait to see Your power working in
great and mighty ways.

....

....

....

....

....

....

....

....

....

....

....

....

....

....

....

....

....

....

....

....

It is good to wait quietly for the salvation of the LORD.

LAMENTATIONS 3:26

Our world is loud. It's busy. It's fast. Silence is a stranger that, so often, we run away from. We put in our headphones, turn on the television, flip through the radio stations. When is the last time you simply let your world go silent? Even when we want to go silent, sometimes silence is out of reach for us with wonderfully boisterous children around the house.

When our days are a roar of constant noise, God's still, small voice tends to get muddled. We stop listening for Him and instead listen to the loudest voices and the most urgent and pressing priorities. We can't hear God's voice when we're filling our ears with everything else.

Dear friend, embrace the silence. Search for it, even if it seems out of reach. Cultivate it, even if it'll take some work. Sit in quiet stillness with the Lord today. It might feel uncomfortable, and you may even feel jittery. You may feel the urge to fidget or scroll through your phone or check the news. You may feel antsy, like you need some noise to fill the void. But it's in the quiet that God's still, small voice is best heard. Silence the noise and listen to Him.

....

Here I am, Lord. I'm stepping away from the noise and listening for Your voice.

So now faith, hope, and love abide, these
three; but the greatest of these is love.

1 Corinthians 13:13 esv

The coffeepot broke. Your child woke up with a cold—or you did. You've yelled at your spouse, and it's not even 6:00 a.m. yet. You forgot to pay a bill, and now you've incurred a late charge. When the morning begins badly, it's hard not to let it affect the rest of your day. But there is good news: even on the roughest of days, the Lord can smooth out a bumpy start.

Try praying on the way to school. Stop by your favorite drive-through coffee shop on the way home. Treat yourself to a movie on the couch with your sick little one. Yelled at your spouse? Apologize with a goofy text or their favorite meal. Rely on God's faithfulness and His power to turn all things to good.

He is the one who turned water into wine, death into resurrection, ashes into beauty, and nothingness into creation. He makes all things new. When your day seems like it's turning into a disaster, call on the Lord. He is faithful to respond.

Father, some days start out so rough, but I know You're faithful in all my days. Help me remember that when things get hard.

....

....

....

....

....

....

....

....

....

....

....

....

....

....

....

....

....

....

....

....

....

....

❧❧❧❧❧❧❧ Day 60 ❧❧❧❧❧❧❧

Let each one give [thoughtfully and with purpose]
just as he has decided in his heart, not grudgingly or
under compulsion, for God loves a cheerful giver [and
delights in the one whose heart is in his gift].

2 CORINTHIANS 9:7 AMP

You've heard it said, "It is better to give than receive." But do you believe it? Do you live it? And why—in this world that tells us getting is more important—should you give? The answer is because our Savior did. Jesus came into this world and gave it all. He laid down His life for us to give us an example of how to live.

As mothers, we tend to give quite naturally to our children. They need a lot from us, and our natural instinct is to respond generously and lovingly. But what about giving to others outside our families? Since we are all so richly blessed, how about experiencing the joy of giving to others today? Even if you feel you have little to give, you have something. If you've been blessed with the joy of the Lord, give a smile. If your table is always full, give a meal. Give whatever you can. Through blessing others, you are acting as the hands and feet of Jesus. You may not receive a thank-you, and you may not even receive an acknowledgment, but you will receive joy. And with it, you'll find contentment for your soul.

....

Father, open my eyes to all the ways I can bless others with what You've given me.

....

....

....

....

....

....

....

....

....

....

....

....

....

....

....

....

....

....

....

....

....

....

Trust in the LORD forever, for the LORD, the
LORD himself, is the Rock eternal.

ISAIAH 26:4

Fear is invisible but extremely powerful. Like a spider's web, it clings to everything it touches. It can be paralyzing, overwhelming, all-encompassing, and life altering. Fear runs rampant in our world, especially in the lives of many parents. There are so many dangers from which we want to protect our children, so many concerns we have for them and their young lives.

But as God's beloved daughters, we do not need to give way to fear. Instead, we can walk in peaceful confidence, knowing that the almighty God of the universe takes care of us. He holds us in the palm of His hand—the same hand that filled the oceans and flung the stars into the farthest reaches of the heavens. He, the one who never grows weary, watches over us while we sleep and commands the sun to rise and greet us each morning. He watches over our precious children— who truly belong to Him and are merely under our care for a while. The Lord our God is greater than all our fears.

Release your fears today. Lay them at the feet of God. Breathe in His promises of provision and exhale any doubt. The Lord is faithful to protect His children. Trust in His faithfulness to you.

....

I give my fears to You, Lord Jesus. Thank You for Your promised relief and peace.

"A new command I give you: Love one another. As I have loved you, so you must love one another."

JOHN 13:34

When was the last time you really enjoyed your family? Really looked at your partner and asked how they are doing? Can you recall the last time you went out to dinner with your parents and basked in their company instead of rushing off to your next commitment? When did you last spend time with your children, not because of a scheduled activity or obligation but simply to enjoy their presence?

Life is short, and with each passing year, the time seems to fly by even quicker. Making time for family and close friends is so important, but with packed schedules and obligations vying for our attention, it often gets pushed to the side.

Be intentional today. Family matters. Friends matter. Push pause on your day, afternoon, or evening and really invest in a family member or friend. Be present and make memories.

....

I get so caught up in everyday life, Father. Help me make my loved ones a priority.

....

....

....

....

....

....

....

....

....

....

....

....

....

....

....

....

....

....

May these words of my mouth and this meditation of my heart
be pleasing in your sight, LORD, my Rock and my Redeemer.
PSALM 19:14

Our words have power. Not only the power to impact someone else but also the power to alter our own thinking. Ponder this: if your words are always full of complaints about life's busyness and difficulties, the hardships and frustrations of raising your children, you're going to begin believing that life is negative.

Why not try a different way? Instead of distress, speak words of hope in the Lord and joy in His faithfulness. Speak words of gratitude. We don't need to pretend things are easy when they're not. But it's important to realize we have control over where we place our focus. When we make an intentional practice of gratitude, we shift our perspective and start to fill our lives with positivity and praise.

When negative words begin springing to your lips, try giving thanks to the Lord instead. When despair creeps into your conversation, declare the truths of who God is and what He says in His Word. Your Lord brings light, not darkness; He brings peace, not strife; and He offers hope, not despair.

....

May the words of my mouth always be pleasing to You, Lord.

Peacemakers who sow in peace reap a harvest of righteousness.

JAMES 3:18

C onflict is inevitable in our broken world. Because Christians are sinners, not every one of our interactions with others is going to be perfect. We will be hurt and we will hurt others—even those we love. Even our kids. It's a hard truth, but there is good news: God uses us as His peacemakers. Romans 12:18 says, "If possible, so far as it depends on you, live peaceably with all" (ESV). While you can't control what others do, you can control yourself.

As far as it depends on you, run toward peace. Choose calm instead of anger, and bring reconciliation to others through your actions and words. If you need to confront others, do so in love and with grace. If you wronged someone—even and especially your child—apologize. Model for them humility and peacemaking. Being a peacemaker isn't passive or weak; it requires a quiet strength that trusts completely in the Lord and in His ways. And it is absolutely needed in our world today, where being right is valued over being kind, where division and discord are rampant.

By embodying the spirit of a peacemaker, you will impact those around you. You will point them toward the God of peace. You will be walking in Jesus' footsteps, just as we've been instructed.

....

Lord, help me rely on Your strength to be a peacemaker in every situation.

Day 65

The LORD will guide you always; he will satisfy your needs in a sun-scorched land and will strengthen your frame. You will be like a well-watered garden, like a spring whose waters never fail.

ISAIAH 58:11

In the morning, before the birds begin stirring and the stars fade into the sky, God is there. He knows the course of your day and is already providing all you'll need for it. His grace is yours before you even get out of bed. If you're feeling tired and overwhelmed, God is waiting for you to turn to Him and hand Him your burdens. If you're excited for this new day, He is rejoicing along with you. This is the day the Lord has made. If you're anxious or concerned, dreading the coming dawn, the Lord is there to comfort you. He is our strength.

You can walk in confidence today—whatever may come—because God is with you. He will be with you each step of the way, through the trying times, the moments filled with laughter, and all those moments in between. Today is a new day, brimming with God's promises and glimpses of His wonder. Go forth with joy into this new day.

....

Your presence in my life is all I truly need, Lord. Thank You for this new day.

"For I am the LORD your God who takes hold of your right
hand and says to you, Do not fear; I will help you."
ISAIAH 41:13

D o you ever hit an afternoon slump? You just ate lunch, you're
feeling a little groggy, and even a double shot of espresso can't
get you going. You may not have time for a two-hour nap—it'll be time
to pick up the kids before long—but what about turning to something
other than caffeine to combat your low energy?

Open the windows and breathe in the fresh air. Walk around outside for a few minutes. Munch on some fruit. Turn on some music and
dance. Do some jumping jacks. Be silly with your spouse, your friends,
or even your pet. Stretch and pray. You'll be surprised how these activities can impact your energy.

When the afternoon slump creeps up again, don't just chow down
on sugar and caffeine; instead, fight it with activity, a healthy snack,
laughter, or prayer. It's a healthy way to boost your focus.

··

When I hit the afternoon slump, remind me of ways I can be energized
instead of discouraged, Lord.

....

....

....

....

....

....

....

....

....

....

....

....

....

....

....

....

....

....

....

*Search me, God, and know my heart; test me and know
my anxious thoughts. See if there is any offensive
way in me, and lead me in the way everlasting.*

PSALM 139:23–24

Have you ever confessed one of your deepest, darkest secrets . . . and then waited with trepidation for a response? Your biggest parenting fail, a long-buried sin of the past, or a trauma you experienced, still tender to discuss. Hopefully, the response was filled with love and grace—for we've all fallen short of God's perfection. But if it wasn't, hear this truth: God already knows all your deepest, darkest secrets—even the worst sins—and He still loves you.

In Psalm 139, the psalmist asked God to search his heart, to know his thoughts, and to lead him. Why? Because he knew that God is a caring God who desires to make him more like Christ. While some believers may simply want God to look at their outward acts of service and compassion, the psalmist asked God to look within.

When you ask God to examine you, He'll show you how to be more pleasing to Him. He'll lead you on the right path, and He'll transform your life inside and out. He will wash you spotlessly clean of every sin. Rest in the safety and certainty of knowing that you are His own beloved child.

....

Lord, test me, examine me, and know my anxious thoughts. Lead me in the way everlasting.

You were taught, with regard to your former way of life, to put off
your old self, which is being corrupted by its deceitful desires; to
be made new in the attitude of your minds; and to put on the new
self, created to be like God in true righteousness and holiness.

EPHESIANS 4:22–24

Just like making your bed or exercising regularly, creating a new habit—such as making time to rest, eating healthier, drinking more water, or devoting more time to prayer—takes practice and commitment. First, you must decide that you both need and want this new habit. Next, you must plan how you will build this habit. Then, take that first step toward completing your plan, and try your hardest to stick to it. Sure, you may mess up along the way, but just get back up and try again and again until the habit is formed. Any and all progress toward your new habit is beneficial.

Life is busy, and it's easy to forgo rest, good nutrition, exercise, prayer time, and any number of other healthy, beneficial practices. But if you've made it a habit, you'll automatically incorporate it into your life. Whether it's carving out a morning quiet time, journaling, praying, or simply committing to sleeping enough at night, good habits will bless you for the remainder of your life.

....

Lord, please give me the discipline to incorporate healthy habits into my
life—for my sake and my family's sake.

....

....

....

....

....

....

....

....

....

....

....

....

....

....

....

....

....

....

....

....

*"Blessed are the peacemakers, for they
will be called children of God."*

MATTHEW 5:9

Have you ever noticed a physical reaction when you're worried? For many, a pounding heart, sweating, shaking, shortness of breath, difficulty swallowing, nausea, and dizziness begin to take hold of the body. It may not be obvious at first, but as your anxiety increases, the physical symptoms become stronger.

Have you felt any of those symptoms this week? Do you feel surprised by how well those words describe you? Friend, this life has many worries, but our God is bigger and stronger than them all.

Take a deep breath. As you breathe in, remind yourself of God's promises and faithfulness. As you breathe out, imagine all your worries flowing out of your body—because where the Spirit of the Lord is, there is freedom. Continue this deep breathing until your body relaxes and the Lord calms you. God is bigger than any trouble or worry; ask Him to fill you with His spirit of peace.

The Lord is with us in our anxieties and frailties. He gently comforts us, graciously gives us peace, and unwaveringly reminds us that He is in control—we are seen and loved, even when worry threatens to overtake our hearts.

....

Lord, I'm often full of worry, but I know You have not abandoned me to this anxiety. Come quickly, Father.

*Let us hold unswervingly to the hope we
profess, for he who promised is faithful.*

HEBREWS 10:23

Moms often have mile-long to-do lists seven days a week, 365 days a year. At the end of some days, do you ever feel defeated by everything you weren't able to accomplish? Even the best-laid plans can fail because life—especially life with children—is often unpredictable and messy. If you weren't able to finish everything you needed or wanted to get done, today can still be a good day; you do not need to feel defeated.

Think about all that you were able to do and to experience today, from the smallest to the largest thing. Maybe you made the bed and put bread in the toaster. You got the kids clothed and to the bus on time—or perhaps you successfully set them up with independent work for homeschooling. You made dinner or mowed the lawn for someone who's sick. You encouraged a friend. You called your mom and shared a laugh. You reassured your spouse. Every day has good in it because Christ is in every day.

Don't allow disappointments to rule your thoughts. Celebrate the good you experience, and thank God for blessing you with another day.

....

*Thank You for being with me, Lord, through the highs and lows of each
day. Help me to focus on my blessings rather than my productivity.*

*No eye has seen, no ear has heard, and no mind has imagined
what God has prepared for those who love him.*

I CORINTHIANS 2:9 NLT

When you hand your child a bowl of ice cream, are they completely satisfied with just one scoop? Maybe they even hand it back and ask, "Can I have more?" Maybe they hand it back six more times and ask for more. It's pretty relatable, honestly. Who doesn't want more ice cream? But how often do we still, as adults, do this with things far more consequential than an after-dinner treat? To us, more is so often equated with better.

What do you want more of today? Money, clothes, beauty products, or electronics? Maybe it's more vacation time, more power, or more prestige. More is enticing, and it promises fulfillment—for a moment.

The next time you begin thinking, *I want more*, rephrase and think instead, *I have more than enough.* You have a God who loves you and a Savior who gave His life for you. You have life and breath and grace. Delight in your God who always gives you more than enough.

....

Father, I often deceive myself into thinking I need more, but You are more than enough. Help me grow in gratitude and contentment.

....

....

....

....

....

....

....

....

....

....

....

....

....

....

....

....

....

....

*And God is able to bless you abundantly, so that
in all things at all times, having all that you
need, you will abound in every good work.*

2 Corinthians 9:8

God will meet all your needs. Yes, all of them. In fact, only He can fulfill your truest and deepest needs for purpose, contentment, peace, and salvation. If dissatisfaction is stealing your peace of mind today, you're not alone. While we live on this earth, we will deal with longing for something that seems unreachable. It's a symptom of being human. God placed a longing within us that only He can fill.

Some people turn to the stuff of this world, to other people, or to jobs or hobbies for fulfillment. Sometimes we even turn to motherhood to search for this fulfillment. And while some things may temporarily bring happiness or distraction—and motherhood is certainly a wonderful endeavor—only God can provide eternal fulfillment. He can satisfy you when nothing and no one else does. That doesn't mean you should give up all your hopes and dreams for happiness on this earth. It simply means that God has more for you, better for you, divinely perfect for you. You can rely on Him to work beyond your understanding. In that truth, there is peace.

Lord, I know that only You can truly satisfy; fill me with Your presence.

The name of the LORD is a fortified tower;
the righteous run to it and are safe.

PROVERBS 18:10

Imagine you're walking down a busy sidewalk. What would happen if you suddenly stopped and sat down to rest right in the middle of the sidewalk? You'd probably get bumped and knocked around. It wouldn't feel particularly restful because you'd be distracted—by the threat of imminent trampling.

That's often how it feels when we try to rest in this busy world. There's just so much going on. We sit down to pray, and the phone rings. We close the door, and one of our precious little ones knocks.

How can you sit still and find peace without getting trampled? First, get off the sidewalk. That means you need to set boundaries and make your times of rest clear. Tell your family. Turn off your phone. Remove distractions, and make it clear you cannot be interrupted, except for true emergencies. This can be really difficult for moms, especially when our children are young. But can you find a creative way to make this happen? Can you and your husband trade off some resting time? When you get off the sidewalk, you can fully focus on being still before the Lord.

You can sit still in a busy world, even when you're raising children who need you—it just takes boundaries and intentional planning.

....

Help me set boundaries so that I may have time to sit still before You, Lord.

....

....

....

....

....

....

....

....

....

....

....

....

....

....

....

....

....

....

Day 74

*The thief comes only to steal and kill and destroy; I have
come that they may have life, and have it to the full.*

JOHN 10:10

When a plant is thriving, it grows healthy and strong, producing flowers, fruit, or vegetables. When a baby is thriving, they are gaining weight, becoming aware of surroundings, and hitting milestones. But what does it look like for you to thrive?

Understand that God wants you to thrive and to live life abundantly. Sometimes, thriving looks like adventure and spontaneity, while at other times, thriving means quiet and stillness and solitude. If you're in a particularly busy season of life, thriving may be having a clear mind and restful spirit.

Instead of striving this week, ask God how He wants you to thrive. And remember that thriving doesn't always mean producing; sometimes it means lounging in an easy chair with a book, taking a leisurely walk in the park, or simply sitting and watching the sunset with your Savior, your spouse, or your children. How can you thrive today?

....

You know what's best for me, Lord. Here I am. Please teach me to thrive.

⊰⊰⊰⊰⊰⊰ Day 75 ⊱⊱⊱⊱⊱⊱

Greater love has no one than this: to lay
down one's life for one's friends.

JOHN 15:13

W e live in a digital world, and often we have a stack of devices
to prove it: laptops, tablets, smartphones, smartwatches, tele-
visions with endless streaming options, an abundant selection of apps
to choose from. Our tech helps us communicate, stay organized, and
meet the many demands placed upon us. We're able to easily record our
children's precious moments with the click of a button. We can scour
the internet for tips and advice on anything and everything. But do you
ever feel like your digital life is pulling away from your real life? Or,
even worse, pulling away from your walk with Jesus?

When you have the world in your hands, it's easy to become distracted. When we use tech as a legitimate tool, it's easy to become numb
to how much time we spend scrolling social media, streaming shows, or
playing games. Would you be willing to lay down some of those distractions to create more time to focus on your spiritual walk instead? Even
thirty extra minutes of time spent with the Lord can leave us feeling
refreshed and focused, ready to tackle our busy lives and carve out more
intentional time for self-care.

....

Lord, help me lay down distractions that are not supporting me in my goal
of serving You and my family, and help me to choose truly edifying self-care
options for my downtime.

150

....

....

....

....

....

....

....

....

....

....

....

....

....

....

....

....

....

....

....

....

Now glory be to God, who by his mighty power at
work within us is able to do far more than we would
ever dare to ask or even dream of—infinitely beyond
our highest prayers, desires, thoughts, or hopes.

EPHESIANS 3:20 TLB

Most people forget their dreams. Even the dreams you have just before waking—you might have a grasp of the details as you move from slumber to reality, but as you become more aware of the real world, the dream fades into the shadows of your subconscious.

Children are better than adults at playing with their dreams. "What do you want to be when you grow up?" "A pirate! Iron Man! Famous!" Ask your kids right now what they want to be when they grow up, and see what they say. Chances are they have big dreams and will say something adorable and quotable.

But then we grow up and stop pretending. We don't imagine or dream about what we could be. We think that to make it in this world, we have to "wake up and smell the coffee." And yes, by settling for the status quo, we'll make it from day to day. But will we truly live?

Close your eyes. Imagine the peace of slumber, letting go of the need to settle for what's expected. Can you remember your dreams, before you had to grow up and be practical? They matter.

....

Lord, thank You for giving me dreams. Help me to recapture the wonder of my dreams.

....

....

....

....

....

....

....

....

....

....

....

....

....

....

....

....

....

....

....

But Moses said to God, "Who am I that I should go to
Pharaoh and bring the Israelites out of Egypt?" And God
said, "I will be with you. And this will be the sign to you that
it is I who have sent you: When you have brought the people
out of Egypt, you will worship God on this mountain."
EXODUS 3:11–12

Do you ever feel like you never quite measure up? Motherhood comes with so many expectations. It can poke at our weaknesses and insecurities. It can trigger a sense of shame or a loss of identity, bringing with it a longing to know and be known.

You may face your days feeling adrift, separated from your roots. And if so, you might find ways to avoid reality, running from who you are, because you feel so unworthy.

But you are not alone. You have been created, so you are connected to your Creator. Who you are measures up because you came from the source of all that matters. You were created to matter. Who are you? Perhaps what matters more is this question: Who are you with?

Lord, thank You for being with me—all the time. Help me remember who I
am in You, even as I pour myself into motherhood with my whole heart.

I know that you can do all things; no
purpose of yours can be thwarted.

JOB 42:2

*Y*ou, dear woman of faith, are full of purpose. Be on the lookout for purpose-killers in your life. They disguise themselves so they can ambush you. They may be obvious like laziness and procrastination. They could wear the masks of self-doubt and distraction. If they're highly clever, they costume themselves in noble detours, such as the unending demands of family, church, and community obligations. These are areas of life that are good in and of themselves but can drop you into a series of excuses that keep you from living your life's purpose.

The things that really matter in this life are always a challenge to pursue and to maintain. Like building good habits, it requires effort not to lose sight of our purpose. That's why so many people—even while pursuing what is good—live lives without purpose. It's so much easier to stay on the simple path. But once you discover and start living out your purpose, you must protect it from an untimely death at all costs.

....

Lord, help me discover my purpose in this life. Place a heavy burden on my heart for everything You want me to be.

Let the wise listen and add to their learning,
and let the discerning get guidance.

PROVERBS 1:5

*H*ave you ever felt like the older you get, the more life you experience, the less you know? If you've ever felt that, it's likely because your perspective of the world is broadening, not that you actually "know less" than you did in years past. And that's a good thing. If anything will throw curveballs at you, reminding you life isn't all figured out yet, it's motherhood. Being a mom requires us to constantly grow, take in new information, and learn new things.

Learning should never stop for any of us, but too often it does. For some, they spend their childhood days in school bored to tears and loathing the thought of more homework or the next test. Occasionally, we'll discover a school subject that inspires us, and for some, this leads to college.

But for many, learning tends to slow down when we reach adulthood. If we allow that to happen, it ends any chance we might have to learn about what matters. Identity. Purpose. Growth. To prevent that from happening, you first need to be curious. Hopefully you're curious enough to discover what else you have to learn.

Lord, thank You for the opportunity to keep learning and growing. Help me continue to broaden my perspective throughout my life.

....

....

....

....

....

....

....

....

....

....

....

....

....

....

....

....

....

....

....

Blessed are those who find wisdom, those who gain understanding.
PROVERBS 3:13

Often, in order to learn, you have to unlearn. We tend to live our lives according to a certain set of assumptions, and if we come across a bit of wisdom that challenges those assumptions, our first instinct may be to resist the new information altogether. This can be particularly true in parenting where, if we're not intentional about our practices, we often simply adopt the patterns we were raised with, conforming to our "normal," repeating what we're used to.

Of course, not every new piece of knowledge will be true, healthy, or worth following. But if you adopt the assumption that there is more for you to learn, a follow-up to that is admitting that some of what you now know could be wrong, or at the very least, could be adjusted.

Here's something you probably already know: not everything in your life is working. That's true for everyone. And when you know something's wrong and are not sure how to make it right, you need to be open to new solutions, new ideas that may challenge your thinking—and perhaps your behavior. You need to be teachable.

....

Lord, help me be open to new ideas. Teach me things You want me to learn—things that honor You and will help me be the best mother and follower of Christ I can be.

....

....

....

....

....

....

....

....

....

....

....

....

....

....

....

....

....

....

....

....

Those who disregard discipline despise themselves, but the
one who heeds correction gains understanding. Wisdom's
instruction is to fear the LORD, and humility comes before honor.

PROVERBS 15:32–33

Road signs are usually helpful. They give us direction, they tell us the speed limit, and they alert us to areas of caution ahead. The sign you probably least want to see says Do Not Enter: Wrong Way. If you see such a sign, chances are you're traveling in the wrong direction and need to take quick action to avoid being mowed down by oncoming traffic.

Nobody likes to receive correction. It's embarrassing. Most often, we simply don't want to believe we need correcting. We're parents now, after all. Full-fledged adults. We're the ones correcting and instructing, right?

Sometimes we even get defensive. We blame others. We accuse the person addressing our errors.

Remember: learning is also about unlearning, and it's unlikely that our journey to what matters—as human beings, as followers of Jesus, as mothers—won't include a few potholes and errant turns onto one-way streets. So take a deep breath. Understand you're human—we all are. And simply turn around and head in the right direction.

....

Lord, thank You for correction, even when it's hard to hear. Help me accept
loving discipline with grace.

If you are wise, your wisdom will reward you.

PROVERBS 9:12

One benefit of pursuing wisdom is that you don't always have to learn from experience. You can save time by avoiding poor choices when you follow good, godly advice.

But experience is still a great teacher. We all make mistakes, even when we're trying our best. Even when we're trying to be excellent mothers and followers of Christ. Experiencing mistakes can be a strong motivator to turn toward wise living. The sting and consequences of past mistakes can be the foundation you needed to fully commit to moving forward into a better, healthier future.

Gaining wisdom, like learning, isn't just about scratching your chin and mulling over cryptic philosophies. It's about living. And you have to step out and live wisdom, placing yourself in the trenches of hard choices between right and wrong, to truly become wiser.

This can be daunting—a little scary, even. Learning in the trenches of motherhood feels like a high-stakes prospect. But what you learn from experience will help you make wise choices in the future. As long as you recognize the opportunity to learn from experience, wisdom will win either way.

....

Lord, help me be open to growing in wisdom through experience, good advice, and Your Holy Spirit.

Whatever your hand finds to do, do it with all your might.

ECCLESIASTES 9:10

Have you ever seen the attention to detail in Shaker-made furniture? Most active during the nineteenth century, the Shakers were a community known not just for quality furniture but also for ingenious inventions such as the circular saw and the washing machine. They also created austere, utilitarian buildings, glorious music and literature, rich agriculture, and a joyful communal life. The Shakers were connected to the quality of God's work in creation, so the focus of their work and lives was to reflect a similar level of quality and excellence in whatever they put their hands to.

As you continue to grow into your identity and purpose as a mother, as you continue to build a life that matters, you'll realize that this all is a reflection of the quality work of your Creator. Whether you are doing chores around the house, homeschooling your kids, rocking your side hustle, tending your Eden-like garden, diving into volunteer work, or any of a thousand other activities, all your work is a reflection of your dedication to the Lord.

You yourself are an intricate, gorgeous work of art. Raise the bar on what you do to reflect who you are.

....

Lord, help me work with all my might, reflecting Your excellence in my life.

....

....

....

....

....

....

....

....

....

....

....

....

....

....

....

....

....

....

~~~~~~~ Day 84 *~~~~~~*

"Be fruitful . . . multiply on the earth and increase upon it."

GENESIS 9:7

If you're reading this book, it's safe to assume you have one or more children. What a calling you have! As mothers, our goal is likely to raise children who will follow in our footsteps and grow up to pursue their identities in God. We want to raise them to become parents who'll want to do the same for their children. And on and on it travels, from generation to generation, a legacy of families loving and serving the Lord.

Each of our lives leaves a mark on this world that will echo even after we're gone. What's your legacy? Is your marriage an example of loving well in faithfulness, trust, and forgiveness? Have you shared the good news with people who know Jesus as a result? Perhaps your friendship has meant the world to others. Every life is like a stone tossed into a pool, creating ripples around it. What kind of ripples are you creating?

It's hard work to live as an example. But it's vitally important, especially for parents. Produce a life that is contagious to others.

....

Father, thank You for the opportunity to create an impact in this world. Help me live as a wonderful example to others.

....

....

....

....

....

....

....

....

....

....

....

....

....

....

....

....

....

....

*The word of the L*ORD *came to Abram in a vision: "Do not be*
afraid, Abram. I am your shield, your very great reward."

GENESIS 15:1

Fear can be a healthy emotion. Sometimes it protects us from danger. You should fear crossing the street without looking both ways. You should fear mountain lions, tornado warnings, and smoking five packs of cigarettes a day.

But fear can also keep you from leaving what's familiar to experience this life of adventure. When you embrace these kinds of fears, you'll find yourself only dreaming of adventure and never actually living it.

Am I good enough? Can I do it? What will it be like? What if I fail? What if I get hurt again?

Naming your fears can make them feel a little less threatening. But once they're named, they must be banished, or at least muted. The adventures you've been called to experience as a mother—and as a person—are more significant than your fears. And more important, the One who calls you to step out the door believes you can do it, and He will guide you and protect you.

....

Father, thank You for calling me to adventure! Help me be brave and banish the fears holding me back.

....

....

....

....

....

....

....

....

....

....

....

....

....

....

....

....

....

....

*By the seventh day God had finished his work. On the seventh
day he rested from all his work. God blessed the seventh day.
He made it a Holy Day because on that day he rested from his
work, all the creating God had done. This is the story of how
it all started, of Heaven and Earth when they were created.*

GENESIS 2:2–3 MSG

If you had one day to yourself, without any obligations, what would you do? Read a book, take a nap, go to brunch with your friends, or hunt for treasures at antique stores? Or perhaps you'd just want to watch TV and order-in food—a rare luxury in your busy life.

Now, imagine doing these things even when you still have all of life's usual obligations. Would you feel guilty? Would you feel the need to justify it or explain yourself?

The truth is moms will always have some sort of responsibility to attend to, but we still need to feed our minds, bodies, and souls. As stay-at-home moms who spend the majority of our time focusing on the needs of others, we need to remember that even God rested from His work. Give yourself permission to do something recreational. It's a needed act of kindness for yourself. Make recreation a priority—in whatever form you need it—and reflect on the goodness of a God who loves His children enough to command them to rest.

*God, sometimes recreation and rest feel self-centered. Please remind me that
it's okay to rest.*

[The LORD's] compassions never fail. They are new every morning; great is your faithfulness. I say to myself, "The LORD is my portion; therefore I will wait for him."

LAMENTATIONS 3:22–24

It's important not to make an eternity out of a temporary feeling. You know the days. It's all you can do to get out of bed or get the kids fed and to the bus stop. You're overwhelmed, exhausted, beaten down, discouraged. Maybe you're even feeling hopeless, like absolutely nothing matters.

Friend, most people have been there. For some, it may be physical and require medication. For others, it may be situational. In any case, we should resist tossing clichés at people who are struggling in this way. "Turn that frown upside down!" and "Suck it up, buttercup!" are not helpful words for those suffering.

But just like seeing your problems from a higher perspective makes them seem smaller, so it is that, although everything in you says that this feeling will never end, you can train your mind to hold on to the truth that it is only temporary.

Life is full of seasons, and some are wonderful. Some are difficult. Morning is coming.

....

Father, thank You for seeing me through the darkest, most discouraging times. Help me hold on until morning.

The plans of the diligent lead to profit as
surely as haste leads to poverty.

PROVERBS 21:5

The car is always in the shop. You can't see your desk through the mountain of mail and bills. You seem to be buying more and more with the credit card. You're always arguing with your spouse or your kids about one issue or another.

Does this sound relatable right now? If so, you're probably living in crisis management. In crisis management mode, our focus is always drawn to putting out little fires. Living intentionally and with purpose is the last thing you could imagine doing. But consider that your car wouldn't break down as much if you regularly changed the oil. Perhaps a few late nights are needed to sort through all that paperwork. Maybe it's time to sit down and write out a budget or talk with a credit counselor. Maybe it's time for a weekly date night and a few weekend getaways or a staycation with the kids to rekindle your closeness and work on your family relationships.

Although it may require a shift in behavior and some sacrifice, focusing on preventive maintenance will free you to focus more on the life that matters most to you.

....

Father, help me get out of crisis management mode and live more intentionally for You, myself, and my family.

I praise you because I am fearfully and wonderfully made;
your works are wonderful, I know that full well.

PSALM 139:14

God created each of us to be unique and wonderful. Our bodies are masterpieces, and they're designed to tell us when we're hungry, happy, sad, anxious, sick, or excited. They also tell us when we're tired.

When we are weary and exhausted, it shows physically. Dark circles appear under our eyes, our eyes sting with strain, our limbs feel sluggish, and our hearts sink when the alarm clock blares or the baby cries. Sound familiar?

When your body is telling you it's tired, what do you do? Do you try to push through and keep going until you reach your breaking point? Or perhaps you ignore the symptoms until you get physically sick. We live in a culture that glorifies busyness, and the life of a stay-at-home mom is legitimately busy. We don't get vacation time or sick days. But at some point, you really need to rest. Honor your body when it signals its tiredness. You are fearfully and wonderfully made. Respect your body and give yourself the rest you deserve.

....

You created our bodies so intricately, Father. Help me honor Your creation with the rest my body needs.

"For my yoke is easy and my burden is light."
MATTHEW 11:30

Taking a relaxing bath after the kids are in bed. Working on a personal hobby. Making time for exercise. Enjoying a cup of your favorite tea while watching the sunrise—or sunset, if you're not an early bird. All these things sound lovely, don't they?

They are all acts of self-care, so often neglected by stay-at-home moms who are focused on taking care of others most of the time. The time, energy, and effort we sacrifice for our children are well spent, but Scripture is clear about the importance of rest—for everyone, and that includes mothers. Scripture is clear that human beings have needs and that God cares about those needs. When the Lord rested after He created Adam and Eve, it wasn't because He needed to rest. Rather He was giving us an example of how to live.

Find joy in that example; take delight in the Lord who knows that we are fragile, in need of frequent rejuvenation. He desires for us to take time for ourselves to recharge and refocus so we can be our best selves for our families. It is not selfish to make sure your cup is refilled as you continually fill the cups of others.

....

Lord, thank You for the gift of self-care, allowing time and space for myself during this demanding season of motherhood.

....

....

....

....

....

....

....

....

....

....

....

....

....

....

....

....

....

....

Oh, the depth of the riches of the wisdom and knowledge of God!
How unsearchable his judgments, and his paths beyond tracing
out! . . . For from him and through him and for him are all things.

Romans 11:33, 36

Much of what truly matters in life is discovered when we wrestle with mystery, the areas of life beyond our understanding. The character of the human spirit is certainly a mystery. Women are often mysterious to men, as men are to women. Teenagers are in their own category of mystery for many parents. Humans are complex and full of unpredictable emotion. All moms can readily affirm this truth.

And then there are the even deeper mysteries: If God exists, why won't He prove His existence? If God is loving, how can He allow evil and suffering? What happens after you die? Perhaps you've even heard some of these questions from your children as they innocently wait for you to answer the greatest mysteries of mankind.

Understanding is important. There are answers out there for many of our questions. But it is in negotiating mystery that we are forced to move beyond ourselves and our limited understandings and into the realm of faith and trust.

So perhaps the ultimate question isn't, "What do you know?" It is, "Who do you trust?"

....

Father, help me to place my ultimate trust in You—always.

....

....

....

....

....

....

....

....

....

....

....

....

....

....

....

....

....

....

In the same way, the Spirit helps us in our weakness. We do not know what we ought to pray for, but the Spirit himself intercedes for us through wordless groans.

ROMANS 8:26

I n our lives as moms, at times we are so busy that prayer becomes an afterthought—an option to exercise when all else fails, we're at the end of our resources, and there's nothing left to try.

But, friend, this is backward—for us in our journeys as mothers or for anyone who loves Jesus. Prayer is putting wonder into words. What is it that you need? Speak to the One who supplies every need. What are you struggling to understand? Trust the One who knows all to reveal it to you. What fears have you tied in knots? Lift them to the heavens and remember He's bigger than any monster under the bed. Thank Him for how He has made the impossible possible, and ask Him for courage when you round the next turn.

Sometimes, what's beyond you feels so overwhelming that you have no words. It's all you can do to drop to your knees and just ask to feel His presence. To know that this God of wonders comes near when we pray and meets our every need. Maybe not in the way we expect. Maybe not on the timetable we'd like. But He is there all the same.

....

Father, help me think of prayer as my first and best option, and help me trust You to answer in Your own way and Your own time.

··

··

··

··

··

··

··

··

··

··

··

··

··

··

··

··

··

Let him sit alone in silence, for the LORD has laid it on him.

LAMENTATIONS 3:28

No TV. No music. No cell phone or tablet. No children. No spouse. No friends. No talking. Close your eyes. What do you hear? Silence.

At first, you'll feel uncomfortable. Okay, you'll feel more than uncomfortable—it may actually feel a bit terrifying. But your mind and your spirit need a break. We all need that sometimes. Relax. You'll realize the noise we're so used to is simply crowding out deeper thoughts and greater peace.

You can still hear a few things. Shutting out the world like this actually allows you to remember they are there. Your breathing, for one. It's one of the most important things you do that you never acknowledge. Take several deep, slow breaths. It's almost like hearing yourself live. If you're outside—birds, lawn mowers, kids playing down the street, a dog barking. Listen for the wind. That's almost like hearing the world live. Sleeping restores your body. Resting your senses while awake restores your soul.

....

Lord, help me to feel replenished by resting my soul. Help me listen to the sounds of life around me.

To the person who pleases him, God gives
wisdom, knowledge and happiness.

ECCLESIASTES 2:26

A lot of stay-at-home moms deal with major FOMO (fear of missing out). The term describes a fear we've all felt at one point or another. When we prioritize our kids' needs, some of our desires might get pushed to the back burner. Some of us left successful careers in order to stay home with our kids.

Sometimes the fear of missing out pushes us to say yes to everything we can—probably more than we should. And then we wonder why we're so burned out and exhausted, pulled in too many directions.

It's hard to say no. But it's a word we need to become more comfortable saying. Saying no doesn't have to be unkind or thoughtless; it can be said with gentleness. And sometimes, the person we must say no to is ourselves. Saying no can open up more space in our lives to say yes to the things that truly matter to us: more time with the Lord, quality time with the family, rest and self-care, and the opportunities we're truly passionate about.

So teach yourself to say no without fear, and intentionally curate the activities you say yes to in your life.

....

Lord, when I say no, I'm afraid I'll miss out on something important. Show
me what is truly important so I can say yes at the right times.

Glory to God in the highest heaven, and on earth
peace to those on whom his favor rests.

LUKE 2:14

I f you've ever been to a big city, such as Chicago or New York, you know that walking down the sidewalks and streets isn't a meandering stroll. The pace is fast—really fast. People are intent on getting to their destinations. That's a stark contrast to the pace of visitors at, say, the zoo. There, you pause every few feet to look at the zebras, lions, or bears. You wouldn't think of rushing through the zoo because you'd miss so much.

So consider this: As you go through your week with your family, do you rush through the days like a city commuter, or do you pause to see what's truly happening around you? Most moms have many commitments to keep. We may even feel like big-city taxi services. And yet, this season of life is filled with so many precious moments—moments worthy of pausing to look around and appreciate the beauty of the journey.

Today, remember to slow down once in a while. Look around and notice your child's laughter. Your baby's new milestone. Your teen's achievement. Pause to look people in the eyes when you speak. Try a slower, more intentional approach to your week.

....

Help me remember that life isn't a race, Lord, and that You want my atten-
tion too.

Those who work their land will have abundant food,
but those who chase fantasies have no sense.

PROVERBS 12:11

Normality gets a bad rap sometimes. If life is to be exciting, it's said, you need to embrace change. You have to shake it up and invite the unexpected. While it is important to challenge yourself and not stay stuck in a rut, you probably face plenty of change and chaos without ever having to seek it out. Most moms do. So you also need to protect, as much as possible, a life filled with . . . dare we say it? Routine.

Children need routine. People with emotional and mental disabilities especially struggle without it. Most adults need it too. The natural world has the occasional upheaval—earthquakes, storms—but most of the time, it runs itself by predictable routines. Every day the sun rises and sets. Every year, the seasons change. We depend on these cycles. And if you're looking with the right eyes, you'll grow to love them. The folding of laundry and prepping of meals, the morning carpool and afternoon homework, your prayer and self-care times. There is a lovely rhythm humming in the ordinary. Learn to embrace it, cultivate it, and cherish it.

....

Jesus, thank You for the ordinary, familiar "normal" You've given to me.
Help me see the beauty in it each day.

Let your eyes look straight ahead; fix
your gaze directly before you.

PROVERBS 4:25

S ome stay-at-home moms immediately embrace their role at home with their children. It comes naturally. They adore it. They soak up each second, grateful for everything from dirty diapers to temper tantrums to forgotten homework. At least it seems that way.

But for many, it's hard to make peace with our roles at home. It's hard not to envy the freedom of our childless friends sometimes. It's hard not to feel frustrated with the exhaustion—or even burnout— when we're up night after night with a colicky baby. If you're parenting children with disabilities or you have multiples, increase that exhaustion.

Whether you feel born for the role or you're fighting through it, friend, you are doing important work. It matters to your children. Staying home is often a big sacrifice, and if you've made that sacrifice, it's probably because God put that calling on your life. Fix your gaze directly before you. Stay focused. Remember the value of what you're doing. It's okay to feel frustrated and exhausted sometimes. It's okay to feel like you're fighting for it. We only fight for things that matter.

....

Lord, I believe You've called me to be home with my children during this
season. Help me embrace my role with grace, focus, and renewed energy.

....

....

....

....

....

....

....

....

....

....

....

....

....

....

....

....

....

....

The light shines in the darkness, and the
darkness has not overcome it.

JOHN 1:5 ESV

*C*hoosing joy is like mining for diamonds. No matter how dark it is, you can find precious jewels if only you'll dig a little. Let's dig for diamonds! List the things you're grateful for. You're alive; you're loved; you can love others. You have been blessed with children. Most likely, you have a roof over your head and food on the table. And that's just a start.

Remembering these diamonds is the key to joy. See the sparkling jewel right in front of you. There's rarely a moment where you can't find some glimpses of light wherever you are. Imagine what makes you joyful. Time with your spouse, sweet kisses from your child, snuggles with your pets, chocolate cake, a large pizza, sleeping in, waterskiing, you name it. Sing a joyful song. Your favorite recent hit, a church hymn, a song from your childhood. Try it. It works! There's no denying the darkness within the mine of this world. It's how you spend your time down here that will determine your joy.

....

Father, help me to find the diamonds You've placed all over my life. Keep me mindful of those blessings!

A cheerful heart is good medicine, but a
crushed spirit dries up the bones.

PROVERBS 17:22

N orman Cousins suffered from an illness that often left him in searing pain. However, he discovered a natural way to address it.

He realized that laughter releases endorphins, a natural painkiller and pleasure inducer, and that as little as ten minutes of strong, deep laughter could give him as much as two hours of pain-free sleep. It is said that laughter is the result of a collision between what we expect and what we don't: outrageous behavior, uncomfortable situations, a joke that sends us in one direction and, with a punch line, sends us reeling in another direction.

Laughter is a natural response to what seems outrageous or impossible. And isn't that often what you face in daily life? The very challenges and absurdities you face are often no different than some ridiculous comedy sketch (and if you make a habit of recording your kids at home a lot, you could probably prove this). Laughter is simply a way to release yourself from the burden of mastering life's absurdities. So have a good laugh. Like Norman Cousins, you may find freedom from the pain.

....

Lord, thank You for the gift of laughter. Help me laugh in the face of absur-
dities and difficulties when they try to overwhelm me.

❧❧❧❧❧ Day 100 ❧❧❧❧❧

You will show me the path of life; in Your presence is fullness
of joy; at Your right hand are pleasures forevermore.

PSALM 16:11 NKJV

Life is meant to be enjoyed. We have the pleasures of family and home, hobbies and friends, church communities and nature graciously given to us to enrich our lives. But the key to enjoying life's pleasures is to make God your chief delight.

God loves you unconditionally. Do you take pleasure in that? God will never quit on you. He'll never leave you. God has a plan for you. Doesn't that fill you with joy? God wants to meet your every need and has given you all He has in the gift of His Son. God is just waiting to show you His mercy. He wants to release you from any hopelessness and shame you may be carrying. God has a life for you beyond what you currently see. Doesn't that fill you with joy?

God has commanded us to be filled with joy, so choose to embrace Him. Embrace the delight only the Lord can bring.

....

Father, thank You for a life filled with large and small joys, from my precious children to the breath in my lungs. Help me to find my greatest, most enduring pleasure in You.